KT-133-584

THE IRISH CIVIL SERVICE

The Irish Civil Service

SEÁN DOONEY

INSTITUTE OF PUBLIC ADMINISTRATION
DUBLIN

COUNTY LIBRARY
TOWN CENTRE, TALLAGHT
ACC. NO.   0902 173715
COPY NO.   TC 100
INV. NO.   1792A
PRICE IR£   7 .
CLASS   351.6

© Institute of Public Administration 1976
59 Lansdowne Road
Dublin 4, Ireland

All rights reserved. No part of this publication may be reproduced or transmitted in any form or by any means, electronic or mechanical, including photocopy, recording, or any information storage and retrieval system, without permission in writing from the publisher.

ISBN 0 902173 71 5

Reprinted 1983

Set in Times New Roman

Made and printed in the Republic of Ireland
by Leinster Leader Ltd., Naas, Co. Kildare

Contents

Preface

It was Jim O'Donnell of the Institute of Public Administration who suggested that I write this book. Since Ian Finlay's pioneering work, *The Civil Service*, published in 1966, had gone out of print, those seeking an account of the Irish civil service had to turn to various sources. References to some of these, and material from them, are contained in the present work.

The book briefly outlines the evolution of the civil service since the founding of the state and indicates the important role that civil servants play in the nation's affairs. It sets out in some detail their part in the making and execution of public policy and illustrates this with examples. The rather complicated grading structure is described (about 1,000 grades for 47,000 people), aspects of recruitment and promotion are dealt with and the principles governing civil service pay and the manner in which this is negotiated are also set forth.

Separate chapters deal with education and training and with the various regulations and conventions which govern civil servants in their employment. This is followed by a description of the role of the newly created Department of the Public Service and of its divisions for general personnel matters, remuneration and organisation.

In the final chapter reference is made to developments arising from the Devlin report in relation to such matters as the separation of the making of policy from its execution; the revision of the grading system; the provision of expanded appellate procedures, including the appointment of an ombudsman; and the installation in all departments of units for planning, finance, organisation and personnel. Other possible developments to which reference is made, derive from changing social and economic circumstances and include the modification of existing practices governing the determination of pay, the employment of women and the general conditions surrounding civil service employment.

The temptation to include personal comment—either critical or commendatory—at certain points had to be resisted because of the constraints which bind all civil servants.

I am greatly in the debt of many people for help given to me. Civil service colleagues in my own Department, Agriculture and Fisheries, in the Department of the Public Service and in the Civil Service Commission provided me with draft material in some cases and in others commented on my drafts. Public service colleagues in the Institute of Public Administration were also helpful. In particular I want to thank Mary Prendergast, the Institute's Librarian, to whom no request is ever too much trouble, who provided nearly all the reference material. Jonathan Williams, Books Editor, made many improvements in the text and with charm and efficiency smoothed the path of the finished work on its way to publication.

I could not, of course, have engaged in this activity without the support of an understanding wife. But, in addition, Clodagh read the proofs and made the index. Lovingly I dedicate the book to her.

Seán Dooney
1 June 1976

Chapter One

The Development of the Civil Service

Under Article 17 of the Anglo-Irish Treaty of 1921, the British government agreed to take the necessary steps to transfer to the provisional government to be elected in Ireland the powers and machinery necessary for it to discharge its duties. The provisional government was duly elected and took office in January 1922. The transfer of administrative services from British to Irish control took place in general from 1 April 1922.

With the transfer, Ireland inherited a complete apparatus of government, both central and local. Some 21,000 civil servants, about half of whom were in the service of the Post Office, opted to transfer. The staffs of the existing departments set up by Dáil Eireann, numbering about 130, also merged gradually with the new civil service. The *Final Report of the Commission of Inquiry into the Civil Service 1932–35* described the impact on the civil service of the change to independence as follows:

> The passing of the State services into the control of a native Government, however revolutionary it may have been as a step in the political development of the nation, entailed, broadly speaking, no immediate disturbance of any fundamental kind in the daily work of the average Civil Servant. Under changed masters the same main tasks of administration continued to be performed by the same staffs on the same general lines of organisation and procedure.[1]

The structure of the new civil service was fundamentally the same as that which had developed under the British administration.

---

1. *Final Report of the Commission of Inquiry into the Civil Service 1932–35* (Dublin: Stationery Office, n.d.), par. 8.

The British civil service was a product largely of developments that had taken place in that country since about the middle of the nineteenth century, following the recommendations made in the Northcote-Trevelyan Report of 1855 and by a succession of other commissions who reported in the intervening years.[2]

In the early days of centralised administration, ministers, secretaries and advisers to the sovereign recruited and appointed their own staffs, who, because of the personal nature of their appointment, were liable to lose their positions when their patron lost his. From the sixteenth century onwards a tradition of permanency pervaded the service, but there was still no question of uniformity. At the end of the eighteenth century there was a large number of departments, most of them very small and all of them staffed as separate units and managed in a variety of ways. As the result of a series of parliamentary campaigns conducted in the early part of the nineteenth century — mainly for reasons of economy — some degree of efficiency and cohesion had been introduced into the staffing of departments by the middle of the century and many sinecures deriving from old offices had been abolished.

Structurally, the pre-Treaty Irish civil service differed from the British pattern in some respects. The formal head of the Government in Ireland was the Lord Lieutenant. Under him, the Chief Secretary was the political head and was usually a member of the British Cabinet. Next in the hierarchy came the Under-Secretary, a career civil servant and permanent chief of the Irish civil service. The large United Kingdom services like the Post Office and the Revenue were branches of the British service with local heads who reported to London while maintaining a liaison with the Chief Secretary. The Irish Offices were a mixture of Departments, Boards and Commissions, with a variety of relationships to each other and to the Irish Executive which consisted of the Lord Lieutenant, the Chief Secretary and the Under-Secretary. Some Departments, like the Department of Agriculture and Technical Instruction, were much like modern Departments of State with a permanent Secretary and higher

---

2. Seán Dooney, "Looking at the Civil Service", *Administration*, XX, 3 (1972), 59–86.

staff but an important feature of the Irish Administration was, to quote the report of the MacDonnell Commission, 1912–1914—'the existence of a complex system of Boards and Commissions whose members, paid and unpaid, share between them much of the higher administrative work.' As an example of the central coordinating system it may be noted that the Chief Secretary was political head of the Department of Agriculture and Chairman of the Local Government Board but his control over many offices was only nominal.[3]

One of the first tasks facing the new Irish administration was to agree on a form of government and on the nature of the machine which would serve it. The Constitution of 1922 provided for a cabinet system of government with ministers having individual and collective responsibility. Existing boards, such as those for Local Government and Education, provided an immediate basis for ministries with such functions; some new ministries, such as External Affairs and Defence, had to be formed. The various arrangements made in this direction were given statutory effect by the Ministers and Secretaries Act 1924.[4] This Act provided for the establishment of eleven departments of state: the Departments of the President, Finance, Justice, Local Government and Public Health, Education, Lands and Agriculture, Industry and Commerce, Fisheries, Posts and Telegraphs, Defence, and External Affairs. Each department was assigned to a minister, to be administered by him. The Act also provided for the assignment to the various departments of the functions and powers of the existing branches and offices of the public service. Thus the business of government in Ireland was assigned on a functional basis to eleven ministers who were individually and collectively responsible for its execution, except where provided by law.

As new departments have been created since then (e.g. the Departments of Transport and Power, of Labour, and of the Public Service), an amending Act has been passed on each occasion.

There were, however, some areas where it was considered

3. *Report of Public Services Organisation Review Group 1966–69* (Dublin: Stationery Office, 1969), Prl. 792, par. 3.1.3.
4. Ministers and Secretaries Act 1924 (no. 16).

desirable that the execution of settled policy should be carried out under the control of commissioners who would be legally independent. One such area was that of recruitment to the civil service, where an independent body of commissioners was set up to ensure that selection for appointment should be by open competition, free from patronage and influence. Another was that of revenue collection, where the administration of the Acts imposing taxation was, in the interests of equity, assigned to commissioners with an independent existence from the Minister for Finance. Other commissioners included the Land Commissioners, the Local Appointments Commissioners, the Commissioners for Public Works and the Commissioner of Valuation. In all cases, however, the staff were to be civil servants whose recruitment was to be subject to the approval of the Civil Service Commission and whose general conditions, like those of all other civil servants, were to be determined by the Minister for Finance.

The Ministers and Secretaries Act 1924 also provides the legal basis for the civil service. Section 2 (2) reads:

The Executive Council shall on the recommendation of the Minister appoint the principal officer [or Secretary as he is continued to be called] of each of the said Departments and each of the said Ministers may appoint such other officers and servants to serve in the Department of which he is the head, as such Minister may, with the sanction of the Minister for Finance, determine . . .

This Act expressed a radically new conception of the administration of public business. Before the Treaty, the main feature of Irish central administration had been the existence of a large number of independent boards of commissioners who undertook a large amount of executive work. Under the new system, this work was transferred to the direct control of ministers, apart from certain areas where impartial conduct of the business had to be demonstrated, and execution, as indicated, was left in the hands of statutory commissioners.

An accepted definition of the Irish civil service is that it consists of that body of persons who are selected by the Civil Service Commission to serve, in a civil capacity, the organs of state defined by the Constitution, namely, the President, the Houses of the Oireachtas, the judiciary, the Taoiseach and his ministers, the Attorney General and the Comptroller and Auditor General. The vast majority serve the Taoiseach and ministers in the various departments of state and, indeed, the term civil service can be roughly equated with the civil employees in government departments. Civil servants are paid from monies provided each year by Dáil Eireann.

A distinction is made between the civil service of the government and the civil service of the state. This differentiation derives from a decision of the Supreme Court that an officer serving in the Office of the Attorney General is not a civil servant of the government but of the state.[5] It was clear from the judgment that this view related to other branches of the civil service not under the direct control of ministers. Accordingly, in the Staff of the Houses of the Oireachtas Act 1959,[6] the Ceann Comhairle (Speaker) of the Dáil and the Cathaoirleach (Chairman) of Seanad Eireann (the Senate) occupy the same role as ministers do in relation to the staff of departments.

The public service comprises more than the civil service and consists of (i) civil servants as already defined, (ii) public servants who are employed in the regional health boards, in local authorities and in state-sponsored bodies, and (iii) the army, the gardaí (police) and teachers.

Up to the end of World War II there was no significant growth in the number of public servants in Ireland and, in particular, there was no dramatic increase in the numbers of civil servants — 25,750 in 1945 compared with 21,000 in 1922. After the war, however, the position began to change. For example, the new Departments of Health and of Social Welfare were set up in 1947 to extend and coordinate activities then being carried out by a number of existing departments. Capital expenditure by the state was greatly increased, with large-scale developments in electricity, air and sea transport, harbours, roads, housing and sanitary services. The need to foster economic activity by state spending also led to extensive capital expenditure on projects such as turf production, land drainage and

---

5. *McLoughlin* v. *The Minister for Finance* [1958]. I.R. pp. 1–28.
6. Staff of the Houses of the Oireachtas Act 1959 (no. 38).

reclamation. A great deal of this activity was carried out by an expanded civil service.

The publication of *Economic Development*[7] in 1958 suggested that the Government must in future be in a position to appraise national resources, define the principles to be followed and set the targets to be reached in the process of national economic development. The acceptance of this thesis by the Government and the issue of the First Programme for Economic Expansion was, perhaps, the most significant event in the history of the Irish civil service in the post-war period.[8]

The range and content of government activities has continued to expand in Ireland, as it has in most other modern states. The regulatory functions (to see that the law was observed and to secure the enforcement of sanctions against those who infringed it), which at one time formed a state's main activity, have now multiplied in size and broadened in scope. Besides those regulatory activities, the modern state has taken on, or has been forced to take on, a wide range of new responsibilities concerning employment, economic growth, balance of payments, health, education and welfare services, the environment, cultural activities, and so on. In Ireland, too, the state plays a leading part in agriculture and industry. In agriculture it is concerned with improving the education and skills of farmers and the living and working conditions of the farming community, improving the physical resources available to farmers, advancing and expanding production, eradicating and controlling disease, securing access to markets on reasonable terms, maintaining high marketing standards and providing research facilities. In industry it is concerned with loans and grants, training and retraining facilities, tax reliefs, protection against unfair competition, and other related matters. The state is intimately involved with the provision of facilities, curricula and standards in primary, secondary and third-level education. People expect more and better education, freedom of opportunity for everyone, reasonable conditions for pupils and teachers, and an examination system seen to be fair to all.

7. Economic Development (Dublin: Stationery Office, 1958), Pr. 4803.
8. *Report of Public Services Organisation Review Group 1966–69*, par. 3.1.11.

In the areas of health and of social welfare, people look to the state to ensure that the needs of the old, the sick, the disabled and the unemployed are not overlooked. The state is expected to play the major guiding, stimulating, coordinating, informational and protective role in such diverse areas as the provision of housing and of machinery for the settlement of industrial disputes; in providing rules governing the legal adoption of children and the safety of workers in factories; in setting standards for agricultural produce for sale and for the clinical testing and manufacture of drugs; in providing weather forecasts and granting patents for inventions; in fostering cultural activities and in the protection of consumers.

When one turns to the infrastructure of energy, transport and communications, or of sanitary services, one finds that these services are all mainly provided by the state, either through government departments, local authorities or state-sponsored bodies. The state is now more actively engaged in international affairs. Scarcely a day passes that readers of the newspapers are not made conscious of the effect which membership of the European Community has on their daily lives and, to a lesser extent, such other international bodies as the International Labour Organisation, the World Health Organisation and the Food and Agriculture Organisation.

All these activities exist side by side with the traditional responsibilities of defence, foreign affairs and the maintenance of law and order, each of which, in the more troubled world of today, presents its own complex problems. The state has to raise and disburse money for all these obligations.

The result of this increase in the activities of government has been, of course, a growth in the number of public servants. So long as the public continues to demand more services from government, so long will that growth (and its cost) be likely to continue. The total number of civil servants in January 1975 was 46,946. (This compares with 36,250 in 1970, 31,675 in 1965, and 28,100 in 1960.) Particulars of the numbers in each department/office are at appendix 1 (pp. 158) which also includes the net estimated expenditure by each department in 1976. Although the term 'civil service' conveys a stereotyped image, in fact it comprises a great variety of different occupations. The term is an arbitrary one. If, for example, the postal and telephone services were excluded, as they are in several countries, the civil service would be reduced by 22,000 people or 47 per cent. For the proper execution of its functions, the government must ensure that it has an efficient and responsible public service to carry out all the tasks that fall to its lot. Under the government, the civil service occupies a key position in the public service, in the formulation and implementation of policies. Surrounding the civil service (which is at the hub of the wheel) are a number of other bodies: local authorities, regional boards and state-sponsored bodies, each playing its own part in the overall activity of national development which is now the prime role of government.

In order to ensure that the civil service, substantially the same as that taken over from Britain in 1922, was suitable and adequate for the efficient execution of the more onerous and complex tasks assigned to it in the modern era, the government established a committee in 1966 with the following terms of reference:

> Having regard to the growing responsibilities of Government, to examine and report on the organisation of the Departments of State at the higher levels, including the appropriate distribution of functions as between both Departments themselves and Departments and other bodies.[9]

One aspect of the work of the civil service which the committee did not comment upon—nor was it asked to—was its impact on the public whom it serves. There is a considerable body of research on that subject which tends to show that, on the whole, the image of the civil service is unfavourable. This attitude may, of course, be endemic in the relationship between people and their government, for civil servants are often called upon to perform duties which the public may not like, such as ensuring that statutory provisions and regulations are fully complied with, that taxes are paid, and so on.

A pilot survey carried out in 1969–1970, under the auspices of the Economic and Social Research Institute,[10] indicates that, when asked how important they thought civil servants were in determining

---

9. ibid., par. 1.1.1.
10. John Raven, "Some Results from Pilot Surveys of Attitudes, Values and Perceptions of Socio-Institutional Structures in Ireland", *Economic and Social Review*, IV, 4 (1973), 533–88.

what happens to the country and how it develops, many people felt that the civil service did not have "all that much influence". On the other hand, these respondents felt that senior civil servants had much more influence than others on what happens in the Dáil.

Another survey on the opinions of Dubliners[11] indicates an attitude of distrust towards government officials and suggests that civil servants do not meet the public in a fair manner. Many of this group did not believe that civil servants were impartial.

The most recent survey in this area[12]—on attitudes to the civil service as a career for school-leavers—(carried out by the Institute of Public Administration at the request of the Department of the Public Service) shows that about two-thirds of school-leavers had little idea of the type of work done in the civil service. Most of them tended to see the civil service as impersonal, anti-individualistic and dull.

In his comments on this general topic, Desmond Roche suggests[13] that the poor public image of the civil service may be due to the degree to which the public is informed about it. The writer hopes that this short work may be helpful in that direction.

---

11. Ian Hart, "Public Opinion on Civil Servants and the Role and Power of the Individual in the Local Community", *Administration*, XVIII, 4 (1970), 375–91.
12. *A Study of Attitudes towards the Executive Officer Grade in the Civil Service* (Dublin: Institute of Public Administration, December 1974).
13. D. Roche, "The Civil Servant and Public Relations", *Administration*, XI, 2 (1963), 104–08.

Chapter Two

The Work of the Civil Service

Although the civil service is not the largest element of the public service, it is in many respects the most important part of it. Its influence extends to the various other parts of that service, such as the local authorities, the regional bodies, the state-sponsored bodies, the gardaí, the teachers, the courts and the army, all of whose activities it impinges upon in one way or another, whether in relation to matters of policy, finance, organisation or personnel management. The civil service operates in a different environment from that of the private sector; it is designed to meet political aims, not to produce a profit. The prime purpose of the entire public service is to serve the public, and the first duty of the civil servant is to help his minister meet his responsibilities to the Oireachtas. He works continuously for, with and under the direction of politicians. The administrative system responds to a complex set of demands articulated through the political system which have no parallel in the private sector.

Government is judged not on its profitability but on its social, political, cultural and economic achievements, subject to some overall limitation upon its total demands for taxation. Since a minister is answerable to the electorate, in the sense that all his actions and those of his officials may be questioned in parliament, the discretion and freedom of action of officials is severely limited and they must act consistently. Many of these unique features are well-known and accepted, even if on occasion they appear to be forgotten. For example, the public criticise the expansion in numbers and costs of the civil service and yet continue to press for more of the services which only the state can provide, such as social welfare, security and health.

The peculiar responsibilities of the civil service have important effects on what it does and on how it does it. Accountability to parliament and to the public is an integral part of the daily life of many civil servants, particularly senior officers. This public accountability brings with it a constant awareness of public involvement in decisions which do not appear at the time of taking them to be of enormous significance, as well as the likelihood of disproportionate publicity for the effects of such decisions or for relatively small errors. For example, there were parliamentary questions and wide press publicity in December 1974 and in January 1975 about the cases of the applicant for a post in the civil service whose appointment was deferred because she was overweight, and the applicant for an education grant whose application was rejected because it was not received before the closing date.[1]

The result of this accountability is that detailed records must be kept, that more decisions are taken at higher levels than appear necessary and that the negotiations and discussions leading to the decisions are closely documented. Because public money is involved, the rules relating to the making and receipt of payments are carefully drawn up and meticulously observed. This occasionally gives rise to what might be regarded as an excessive checking and counter-checking of even small financial transactions.

Public accountability also necessitates more centralised arrangements for financial control than are found in the private sector. Few public servants are unaware of the role played by the Department of Finance in relation to the spending of money on various projects; nor are they ignorant of the role of the Department of the Public Service in relation to matters of staff numbers, pay and conditions of service.

Much of the work of the service has no commercial counterpart. Drafting and applying legislation, taking steps to preserve the environment and arranging for the certificate examinations in secondary education, are typical examples of tasks which are unique to government. The success of this work can be evaluated only by standards which are equally unique. This lack of directly comparable work partly explains the relative isolation of civil servants. Besides, they are increasingly the recipients of much confidential information of a social, financial or technical kind which demands the cultivation of

1. *Dáil Debates*, Vol. 276, No. 7, col. 1107, 5 December 1974; *Dáil Debates*, Vol. 277, No. 6, cols. 972–73, 23 January 1975.

a certain detachment and reserve. This sense of comparative insularity is reinforced by the fact that most civil servants spend their entire careers in the civil service.

In all areas of Government activity, judgements exercised by Civil Servants, even at a quite junior level, may involve such intangibles as equity, political acceptability, strategic considerations and even aesthetics. The over-riding emphasis on equity and impartiality is marked in all aspects of Civil Service work.[2]

An important aspect of the Irish civil service is that, although politicians and ministers change, the civil service is permanent. There is something of a paradox in this, in that the civil service is at one and the same time the permanent servant of the state and also the servant of the administration which is for the time being in power.

Although the civil service is numerically exceeded by the state-sponsored bodies sector, which includes such large employers as Córas Iompair Eireann (the state transport authority), tne Electricity Supply Board, Bord na Mona (Irish Peat Development Authority) and Aer Lingus (the state airline), civil servants, as direct employees of ministers and because of the close proximity in which they work with ministers, hold a key position in the formulation and implementation of the various policies for the social, cultural and economic development of the country. The Devlin report suggests that the role of the civil service is of a three-fold nature: policy/advisory, managerial and executive.[3] If one were to generalise, one might say that policy is formulated at the higher levels, that the execution of settled policy (i.e. ensuring that the decisions made by ministers are given effect) is carried out mainly at a lower level, and that managerial functions are exercised by civil servants at practically all levels. Sir William Armstrong, who was head of the Civil Service Department in Britain for several years, summarised the position in the following terms:

---

2. *The Civil Service. Vol. 2. Report of a Management Consultancy Group: Evidence Submitted to the Committee under the Chairmanship of Lord Fulton 1966–68* (London: HMSO, 1968), par. 27.

3. Op. cit., par. 12.2.3.

I believe it to be the main duty of the Civil Service, at this particular point of contact with Ministers on the formulation of policy and the taking of policy decisions, to be the eyes and ears of Ministers, to present to them a picture of ongoing reality, and to work out for them . . . the various alternative policy options open to them and the likely consequences of a choice of any one of them. I believe that to do this job in the way that it ought to be done requires long training and experience, and detailed knowledge of the administrative processes involved, as well as the past history of the subject, of a kind which can only be acquired from a career in a permanent service. I also believe that the chief danger to which politicians and Ministers are exposed is not, as is often supposed, that obstructive bureaucrats will drag their feet in implementing their schemes, but that their own optimism will carry them into schemes and policies which will subsequently be seen to fail—failure which attention to the experience and information available from the Service might have avoided.[4]

The process of formulating policy is variously defined. R. G. S. Brown cites Nevil Johnson's definition:

. . . 'analysing the problems, defining the issues they present, and finding out what methods might be used to deal with them.' This entails making available to the Minister all the special knowledge and techniques that are thought most relevant to the issue under consideration. Since no decisions would be made if *all* relevant considerations had to be sought and taken into account, it also involves the selection and evaluation of different aspects of a problem.[5]

Nevil Johnson himself points out that—

Policy-making occurs in the determination of major objectives,

---

4. Sir William Armstrong, *The Role and Character of the Civil Service* (London: Oxford University Press, for the British Academy, 1970), pp. 13–14.
5. R.G.S. Brown, *The Administrative Process in Britain* (London: Methuen and Co. Ltd., 1970), p. 33.

in the selection of methods of achieving these, and in the continuous adaptation of existing policies to the problems which face a Government. Four features at least of this process need to be stressed. Policy-making is very much concerned with bringing about changes, with altering one's course. In an open society it will involve argument and criticism: indeed the likelihood of public argument is one of the criteria used to decide whether an issue is one of policy. A third point is that we cannot make a clear division between administration and policy-making: administration is a dynamic process from which policy issues constantly arise. Finally, policy-making can be negative, a decision to avoid change and to go on as before.[6]

Ira Sharkansky describes policy-making as encompassing

. . . the formulation, approval and implementation of government programmes. It joins public administrators to numerous other actors who have a stake in policy; these include officials in other branches of government, private citizens, interest groups, political parties, and sometimes the spokesmen of foreign governments. Also, within the policy process are the ideas, resources, stimuli and constraints which influence the participants. The policy process is dynamic and is affected by intense controversies.[7]

In general there are now three main sources of policy: the political, the administrative, and the external, i.e. membership of international bodies, of which perhaps the most obvious example is the European Community. As regards the political source, a minister may take office with a policy already settled—with an objective which his government has an electoral mandate to attain. During his term of office, other political reasons may arise to cause the introduction of a new policy or the modification of existing policy.

Illustrating the administrative source of policy, T. J. Barrington writes:

---

6. Nevil Johnson, "Who are the Policy-Makers?", *Public Administration*, XLIII, 3 (1965), 282.
7. Ira Sharkansky, *Public Administration: Policy Making in Government Agencies* (Chicago: Markham Publishing Company, 1970), p. 3.

. . . a considerable part of modern policy-making arises within the public machine itself, is presented for decision to whatever government happens to be in power and, when it has been decided upon according to whatever value system the ruling party may have, is sent back into the machine for implementing. One can go so far as to say that, given the nature of the responsibilities of the modern State, it is the *duty* of public administrators to identify problems, to solve them, to propound the solutions, and so formulate the material for policy-making on which political decisions will be made. . . . This is not to exclude others from propounding solutions, or to seek to do anything but extend the range and quality of public discussion: but it is to pin a clear load of responsibility on administrators to work out and present solutions to problems of national importance.[8]

Examples of the external sources of policy are the harmonisation of practices to conform with those in operation in the other countries of the European Community, as in the making of revised regulations dealing with road haulage; the decision of the Court of Justice that discrimination may no longer be practised against non-nationals in the awarding of contracts; the disbandment of An Bord Grain (the grain board); and the substitution of the Community price support system for that previously in operation for many agricultural commodities.

If one were again to generalise about the political and administrative sources of policy, one might refer to the reports of commissions of inquiry set up by the government or by individual ministers to advise on specific problems; to comments in the Dáil or Senate or in the newspapers; to changing social and economic conditions; to the activities of pressure groups of various kinds; to reports from inspectors dealing with local administration; to the examination of statistics and other normal management information; to suggestions made by special planning units or 'think tanks' within departments, and to reports of research institutions.

The ideas, suggestions, recommendations and plans are examined and evaluated by the civil servants in the departments

---

8. T. J. Barrington, "Administrative Purpose," *Administration*, XIII, 3 (1965), 179.

concerned. In their analysis, costing and general discussions, civil servants, no matter how sympathetic they may be to the theories and enthusiasms of the advocates of change, and even where they themselves see things needing to be done, must be alive to the wide variety of constraints of a social, financial, economic or other nature, which exist both internally in their own system and externally in the society they serve. In the majority of cases, each matter is submitted, after examination, to the minister for his consideration and decision.

Thus the decisions of a minister are considerably influenced by what goes on before and ministers appreciate that the quality of their decisions depends greatly on the efficiency and resourcefulness of their administrative machinery, on the nature of the official advice they receive and on the thought that informs that advice. The calibre of mind that civil servants bring to their appraisal and analysis of the facts of a specific problem influences, and often determines, the character of a minister's decision. The nature of the policy-making process illustrates the necessity of official advisers of ability, integrity and independence of thought. It is desirable that their outlook be fresh and receptive and that they be conversant with modern techniques and ideas. Sir Edward (now Lord) Boyle, who held a variety of ministerial posts in Britain, had this to say about policy-makers:

Officials with their experience can do a number of extremely important things. They can warn Ministers of criticism to which a policy will render him liable. . . . They can point out to Ministers the snags they may not have thought of . . . with their long experience, officials can encourage or can warn on the merits of some proposed policy . . . on a great many issues Ministers will naturally ask officials for their views, and this will include views on a number of matters which involve political or value judgements . . . in all departments Ministers will have a relationship with their senior advisers, with the heads of branches, and with Under Secretaries, in which no-one feels 'estopped' from expressing their views freely. . . . They are the officials who work at the point where policy and administration fuse. They are both responsible for policy within their branches and in touch with day to day administration; they are particularly key people. . . . Ministers need all the expertise they can get, and if discussions on policy matters between Ministers and officials are to be fruitful, each side has got to do its work. These discussions work much better if both sides are pulling equally. . . .[9]

The Devlin report referred to the considerable volume of work placed on a minister. As a parliamentary representative he has

. . . the usual spate of representations from constituents . . . the customary appearances at public functions in his constituency, while, as a Minister, he will also have a formidable list of requests to attend meetings of various national bodies . . . he must also attend government meetings and brief himself on all items involving government policy even when his Department is not involved and a large proportion of his time must be spent in the Dáil. . . . Where new legislation arises, the volume of government and Oireachtas work may be considerable. On top of all this the normal work of the Department goes on. The public are aware of day-to-day items when matters reach the stage of the Parliamentary Question but this is only the tip of the iceberg.[10]

Many decisions fall to be taken by the government itself. In particular, matters which require the passing of legislation to give them effect must be submitted for government consideration. In addition, where a minister feels that a matter is one of such importance or interest that the government should know of his proposals (or where it impinges on the functions of another minister), he will bring it to the attention of the cabinet and seek its approval for whatever course of action he has in mind.

To ensure that the advice offered to his minister is the best available, a civil servant must keep up-to-date on the subject area of his work and know what is happening in that area in other countries; he must be familiar with current literature on the subject and be

9. Sir Edward Boyle, "Minister or Civil Servant?", *Public Administration*, XLIII, 3 (1965), 255–56.
10. Op. cit., par. 7.1.3.

alive to the people or groups to be approached for information, advice and support. This may necessitate extensive reading, meetings with interested or knowledgeable bodies, discussions with colleagues in his own department, in other departments and in other parts of the public service. It may require dealing with special interest groups. It is difficult to think of any activity that has not got its organised or unorganised group anxious to have decisions taken which will accord with the group's own wishes. One has only to think of the fields of teaching, medicine, industry, and agriculture, to realise the pressures which the groups representing various aspects of these interests bring to bear on the departments concerned. It is the task of the civil servant to endeavour to reconcile the various groups' demands with the common good, to ensure that no group succeeds in obtaining a larger slice of the national cake than it deserves, merely because it is vocal, powerful or rich. The civil servant must have a deep knowledge of his subject, be able to persuade and to reconcile, be neither too intransigent nor yet too ready to concede, perceive wherein the public interest lies and have the determination to safeguard it.

When a decision is taken by a minister or by the government, the civil servant must throw all his energies into the execution of the policy decided upon, irrespective of whether or not it accords with his own recommendations. The position of British civil servants in this regard (and the position is similar for Irish civil servants) was referred to by Harold Wilson when announcing, as Prime Minister, to the House of Commons in February 1966 the appointment of the Fulton committee of inquiry into the management of the British civil service. He said that the government's willingness to consider changes in the civil service did not imply any intention on its part to alter the basic relationship between ministers and civil servants:

> Civil servants, however eminent, remain the confidential advisers of Ministers, who alone are answerable to Parliament for policy; and we do not envisage any change in this fundamental feature of the parliamentary system of democracy.[11]

---

11. *Parliamentary Debates* (House of Commons), Vol. 724, No. 43, Col. 210, 8 February 1966.

The relationship between the civil servant and his minister is one on which the former is publicly silent and the latter generally has little to say. However, ministers are usually willing to acknowledge their debt to their advisers, as Boyle has recognised. The extent of the debt can be deep and complex. Maurice Wright notes that

It is now on record that there are 'no rules, understandings or conventions' limiting the help which civil servants may give to their Ministers in Parliament. It is professionally ethical for civil servants to write speeches, prepare briefs, supply material for answers to Parliamentary Questions, write answers to Parliamentary Questions, and generally to provide information for the Minister to forestall, deflect or disarm criticism from the Opposition.[12]

In the course of their work advising ministers and seeing that decisions are implemented, the types of task which fall to be performed by civil servants are many and varied. Some typical examples of such work are outlined below.

Legislation
When legislation is required to implement some new policy or to change an existing policy, usually one of the senior officials in the field of work where the new measures are to be taken is entrusted with the task of preparing a background memorandum setting out why the legislation is necessary: why the present position in regard to the matter at issue is regarded as unsatisfactory, what benefits will accrue from the passing of the legislation (and what disadvantages, if any), what parties/activities are likely to be affected and in what respects, what changes will be required in existing cognate activities as a result of the new legislation, what the cost will be, and so on. When this memorandum is approved by the minister, it is circulated to other departments which are likely to be concerned and is always sent to the Departments of Finance and of the Public Service. When the views of all the departments have been received, they are incorporated in the final memorandum for submission to the government,

---

12. Maurice Wright, "The Professional Conduct of Civil Servants", *Public Administration*, LI, 1 (1973), 7.

so as to give all the necessary information to enable it to make a decision.

When the government has decided that the legislation is to be proceeded with, the civil servant who has been dealing with the matter writes to the Attorney General, sending him a copy of the memorandum to the government and also the heads of the proposed bill, with a request that the parliamentary draftsman put it into legal form. During the whole of these procedures, the official frequently reports to his superiors on progress and seeks their advice when necessary. When the draft bill is ready, it is carefully examined to ensure that all the departments' requirements have been met. It is then resubmitted to the government, after which it is presented by the minister concerned to the Dáil or to the Senate where it is given several readings. The first of these readings is generally a formality: to obtain permission to introduce the bill for debate. For the second reading, the minister is required to make a formal speech setting out the reasons for the introduction of the bill and outlining its contents. The civil servants concerned accompany the minister to the Dáil for the debate, where they sit in the space reserved for officials; they are not, of course, permitted to take any active part in the proceedings. They take notes of the various points made by deputies in the course of the debate and carry out any further inquiries or research that are necessary, so that the minister will be fully briefed when he comes to make his concluding remarks on this reading of the bill. On occasions when the debate on the reading is completed on the same day, there may be little time for more than perhaps a whispered discussion between the minister and his officials. For each succeeding stage of a bill in its progress through the houses of the Oireachtas, substantially the same procedure is followed: the civil servants attend each house with the minister when the debate is taking place, make notes and inquiries, follow up points made or supply the minister with material for reply, as the circumstances dictate.

Implementing Decisions

A number of further matters must be attended to when legislation is passed by the Oireachtas (or, otherwise, when decisions are taken by the government) which calls for the introduction of new schemes or changes in existing schemes, such as changes in social welfare legislation, the provision of subsidies on food (as was announced in the June 1975 budget statement), or the scheme of assistance, under an EEC directive, for farmers in the disadvantaged parts of the country. For example, the civil servant may need to consider publicity measures such as (i) newspaper/radio/television advertisements, (ii) distribution of leaflets or other publicity material, (iii) local lectures to the general public or to special groups, (iv) a nation-wide address by a minister. It may be necessary to consult with interested parties, or with individuals and groups who are likely to be affected by the decisions (if this has not already been done), as to the most acceptable or most efficient means of implementing these decisions.

If the project has not already been costed in detail, it will be necessary to estimate the administration costs, the amount to be paid out in grants or subsidies or on the purchase of equipment or materials. It will be necessary also to determine how the operation is to be run, whether it will be administered locally or centrally, whether on a functional or geographical basis and what categories of staff are required. The project must be organised to run as economically as possible. Consideration must be given to the location of staff, to their accommodation, to any equipment which they will require, and to other relevant matters.

The civil servant must consider whether any special forms are required, such as application forms, forms stating that certain activities are completed, forms for obtaining statistical information, or forms required for the making of payments. Adequate checking and payment procedures must be decided (if the project is of that nature) and care taken to ensure that public funds are properly recorded and spent. Consultations will be necessary between the officials administering the particular project and their colleagues in the personnel, finance and organisation divisions. All staff must be adequately trained and there must be provision for the free flow of information between them. There must also be a system for providing management information. It is necessary that the senior officers be in a position to examine the operation critically, at all stages, to see whether it is effective or whether any modifications are called for, or if it has served its purpose and may be discontinued. If the project is likely to give rise to correspondence from public representatives, or to a steady flow of parliamentary questions, a system for answering these must be established.

Parliamentary Questions

Scarcely a week of any parliamentary session passes when a minister is not required to answer parliamentary questions about matters relating to the activities of his department, whether of broad policy or of detail. The procedure for dealing with such questions is that the deputy requiring information from a minister formally in the Dáil gives his question to the staff in the Dáil office who transmit it to the private office of the appropriate minister. From here it is sent to the senior officer in charge of the work to which the question relates—this is normally the principal in charge of that division. The standing orders of the Dáil prescribe that a question must reach the Clerk not later than 11 o'clock on the third day preceding that on which it is to be asked, so a reply must be prepared speedily. The civil servant must therefore give the question his immediate and urgent attention. Usually he will be in a position to write the first draft of the answer forthwith, but, in addition, he will have to write a note for his minister's information. This will be a statement setting out the background to the question, what previous questions (if any) have been asked on the same subject, what action has been taken or is being taken in the matter, and so on. In the note he will try to provide information for reply to any supplementary questions which may be asked by the questioning deputy. Civil servants are required to exercise extreme care in dealing with parliamentary questions. As far as the actual reply is concerned, it is generally concise and addressed precisely to the question asked; the note, too, will be concise, yet clear.

Meeting Deputations

Practically every day, one or more deputations, representing the various interests that form part of our pluralist society, are received in each government department. These represent bodies or groups anxious to press their views on ministers and officials and to seek information or action on particular matters which affect them. They range from consumer associations to farming bodies, from trade union representatives to conservation groups, from professional associations to residents' groups. They will not all expect to be received by the minister himself. Often, because of the immense volume of work which devolves on a minister, these interest groups will be received by his senior officials who will listen carefully to their views and discuss the issues. Even on the occasions when the minister is available to see such groups, he will often be accompanied by his officials, who will have briefed him beforehand on the department's views on all aspects of the matter at issue.

Economic Forecasting

Civil servants who advise the Minister for Finance on the state of the economy and on the specific policies to pursue, make economic forecasts of the likely course of the economy over the following year or, in the case of economic programmes, over the following four or five years. They must collect and put together data on various aspects of economic activity, such as employment, production and savings. Most of this data comes from the Central Statistics Office, but often other sources, such as the Confederation of Irish Industry, the Economic and Social Research Institute and the Central Bank produce supplementary figures. These figures have to be analysed and interpreted carefully. The civil servants concerned must be familiar with techniques of statistical and economic analysis and must keep abreast of the latest developments in these fields. In addition, it is important that they maintain a wide range of contacts in the institutions mentioned and further afield in international organisations.

Since forecasting for a current year often presents too short a horizon for most purposes, forecasts have to be produced covering periods of up to five or ten years or even longer. This entails extending into the future trends observed over similar periods in the past and modifying assumptions about expected changes in the future. In the interests of consistency, these exercises may require the use of an econometric model—a series of relationships between aspects of economic activity in the past which can be modified to take account of expected changes in the future (including changes in government policy)—thus enabling an assessment to be made of the effects of such changes on the economy for some period into the future. For the civil servants concerned, this requires further specialised knowledge of statistics and econometrics.

Despite all of this, different interpretations may be put on the same results, so the civil servant must be able to brief his minister, not only on his own conclusions, but also on the work of other institutions which produce different results.

Membership of Committees

Civil servants from different divisions of the same department may be formed into a committee to resolve or recommend on a particular problem which is solely within the jurisdiction of their own department. They may also join colleagues from another department or departments on interdepartmental committees, of either an *ad hoc* or of a standing nature, to make recommendations to a particular minister, or perhaps to a sub-committee of the cabinet, on a subject in which their various departments may have a common interest. An example of the former type is the committee set up in November 1974, comprising representatives of the Departments of Labour, Industry and Commerce, and Transport and Power, to carry out a review of safety measures in Dublin's dockland because of a number of major fires there.[13] Examples of the latter are the committees dealing with agriculture, energy, the environment, fiscal harmonisation, trade, transport, industrial policy, regional policy and social policy in the context of membership of the European Community. Each committee is chaired by the representative of the department with primary responsibility for the subject.

Civil servants may also serve on committees which include persons outside the civil service: public servants from the local authorities, officials from state-sponsored bodies, or members of the public representing pressure groups or other general interests. For example, officers of the Department of the Public Service are members of the national Employer-Labour Conference.

Interview Boards

At various times during their career many senior civil servants will serve on boards to interview persons seeking an initial appointment or a promotion. These boards are set up by the Civil Service or Local Appointments Commission or within the appropriate departments. Their job will be to study the reports on the persons coming

---

13. See *Evening Press*, 7 November 1974.

before them for interview and, in the light of their personal experience of the requirements of the posts to be filled, to assess the abilities and general suitability of the candidates and to make recommendations for the ultimate approval of the minister making the appointment.

Organisation and Personnel

All senior officials participate in these two activities. The extent of an official's involvement depends on the nature of the activity for which he is responsible and the number of staff under his control. His job is to see what tasks lie ahead, what resources will be required to undertake these, and to make advance plans accordingly, usually in consultation with the organisation and personnel divisions of his department. The officers in the latter divisions are, of course, actively involved in these two activities as part of their normal work and, in addition, are engaged in career planning, training and development, disciplinary matters, promotion and management techniques, including systems analysis, operations research and automatic data processing.

Minister's Private Office

Since a minister is preoccupied with important, onerous and time-consuming duties, he relies on his private secretary and the other staff of his private office to ensure that his routine, day-to-day responsibilities are attended to promptly and efficiently. For example, a minister will not normally have time to write replies to more than a few of the many letters he receives each day. For the remainder he depends on his private secretary to have the matter investigated and a reply prepared for his signature. When the minister requires background information for meetings, speeches, interviews and Dáil debates, his private secretary collects this material and ensures that the minister is properly apprised.

The minister's office also acts as a channel through which work flows to him from his department, and vice versa. All submissions from the department requiring ministerial authorisation are sent to his private office. The private secretary communicates the minister's view to the department officials concerned.

State-Sponsored Bodies

When a decision has been taken by a minister or by the government that a state-sponsored body should be set up to undertake some new service, the task of arranging for the establishment of the body is assigned to a senior officer. If not already decided, he has to consider and obtain ministerial approval or direction about whether it is to be established by statute (as a statutory corporation) or as a public or private company; how the board is to be constituted and remunerated; whether the members should be appointed by the minister or on the nomination of appropriate organisations; whether the enterprise will rely on the state for its finance or will itself be able to provide all, or part, of its needs. He also has to consider what other provisions should properly be included in the legislation or articles of association. There will be consultation with the Department of the Public Service on staffing and other relevant matters. Ministerial control of all state-sponsored bodies on matters of basic policy is usually discussed by the minister directly with the board, but the civil servant often has daily contact with officials of the body, arising from representations made to the minister, from parliamentary questions, and from suggestions for amending legislation affecting the organisation's activities; in particular, he will have discussions on capital and current expenditure. If the body is receiving financial grants from the exchequer, the civil servant consults with the Department of Finance.

The extent of the involvement of a minister and his department in the affairs of a state-sponsored body depends on the nature and range of activities undertaken and is limited by the established convention that ministers do not intervene in the day-to-day affairs of such bodies. In general, the civil servant from time to time takes part in the reappointment by the minister of the chairman and members, some staff matters, the organisation of superannuation schemes, and any significant extension of activities, particularly those which might incur major expenditure. It is, of course, a particular duty of the civil servant to keep the minister informed about progress and development in order to ensure that the policies laid down by the Oireachtas and the minister are being adhered to by the body.

Local Authorities

A number of departments (Local Government, Agriculture and Fisheries, and Education) have local authorities under their aegis. In each of these departments there are one or more divisions, comprised of general service officers who work in close liaison with their technical counterparts, dealing with the various aspects of their department's relationships with its local authorities. For example, the technical education division of the Department of Education deals with the vocational education committees. These authorities operate under a body of law which since the turn of the century, and even before, has been designed by the different controlling departments.

In the main, the relationship embraces (i) matters relating to the numbers and grading of staff and their conditions of appointment, pay and superannuation, (ii) questions of finance, since all local authorities derive a considerable part of their income from state grants, and (iii) the revision and amendment of legislation arising from the development of existing services or the provision of new services by the local authorities. Policy is almost invariably made in the departments, though, of course, the local authorities participate in its formulation. For example, policy in relation to environmental planning or to housing is made in the Department of Local Government. A policy is frequently communicated to the local authority by a circular letter and is amplified and explained, where necessary, at meetings between officers of the central department and the local authority. Sometimes, schemes designed to give effect to the policy are formulated in the department and then transmitted to the local authority for implementation. Usually these schemes provide for set procedures and indicate the degree of local autonomy under which they are to be operated. In some cases the adoption of the schemes rests with the local authorities themselves.

The departments are thus in a strong position to influence the activities of their local authorities although, of course, the degree of their influence depends on the terms of the governing legislation and on tradition and practice. While it is true that the authorities generally operate with a strong sense of responsibility, it is nevertheless occasionally necessary for a central department to exercise its powers of persuasion to induce the local body to adopt and operate a scheme; the central department has controlling power over financial grants and the appointment of staff. The statutes governing the activities of local authorities are, on the whole, specific, unlike those in force in many other European countries. (In Ireland a local authority may not, in general, undertake a function or power unless specifically authorised to do so. In many other countries, it may exercise any function or power which is not controlled or prohibited by central authority.) Hence, local authorities frequently require the consent of the controlling department before taking some specific action. The minister's approval to the action proposed, whether in its original or in an amended form, can be given only when the department has closely examined the proposal.

Attendance at International Meetings
In recent years the Irish civil service has participated more frequently in the work of international agencies. Nevertheless, up to Ireland's accession to the European Community, the number of home-based personnel involved in work of this kind was small and these few were invariably the envy of their colleagues.

Things have changed. Any officer from middle management grade upwards is now liable to find himself seated around a table in Brussels as a member of an Irish delegation or even as spokesman for it. He will be confronted by colleagues from the other eight member states and probably also by civil servants of the Commission itself. The situation will vary from the lowly *ad hoc* working group to the heady atmosphere of a Council of Ministers or a summit meeting.

In a typical instance, the Commission invites member countries to bilateral discussions on some idea it hopes to put forward. Here is the first chance for the national civil servant to advance his country's interest by influencing the Commission's thinking. After bilateral discussions, the Commission puts its ideas into the draft text of a regulation or directive for examination by a working group set up by the Council of Ministers.

The working group will not only examine the principle and objectives of the proposal but will scrutinise the text word-by-word, thus determining the eventual shape of the measure. The delegate to a group is inevitably faced with making instant decisions, exercising his own judgement on when to agree, when to compromise and when to insist.

Next the proposal is considered by high-level permanent committees. These committees are expected to resolve most of the conflicts and qualifications of the original working group. Finally the proposal comes before the Council of Ministers. To attend a Council meeting as part of his country's delegation is invariably an exciting experience for the civil servant, who has up to then represented his country at official level on one particular issue. At this stage, the minister is his country's spokesman and much depends on the briefing given him before and during the meeting to enable him to support his arguments or to counter those of other ministers. The civil servant has therefore a key role to play even in these final negotiations.

In each functional area of the Commission's activities there are several regular and *ad hoc* meetings of one kind or other which must also be attended. The demands on the officer attending are always the same: thorough knowledge of the subject; ability to take quick decisions and to respond to particular proposals; negotiating skill to realise when to stand firm, when to concede and when to support an alternative viewpoint.

Apart from the activities within the Community, the older international bodies like FAO, UNESCO and OECD continue with their work, usually in a wider international field. The work of these organisations may not have the same dramatic content or the immediate impact on people's daily lives that the European Community has, but they are each important and the demands on the civil servants who must attend their meetings are no less challenging.

Civil servants representing their country must be forever conscious of the fact that their ability and decorum at international meetings have an important bearing on their country's reputation and standing abroad.

The type of work done by higher civil servants was well summarised by William Reid, himself a senior officer, at a careers symposium in Britain:

You will spend a fair amount of time in your office writing and answering letters to members of the public, other civil servants, outside bodies with which your department deals; preparing memoranda, writing minutes, suggesting how to initiate, implement or alter policy; telephoning or being telephoned; interviewing visitors; discussing informally with colleagues how or what to do; consulting the specialists with whom the Administrative civil servant has more and more contact: architects, surveyors, engineers, cost accountants, doctors, inspectors of several kinds. In many departments of government Principals and some Assistant Secretaries have territorial responsibilities which necessitate periodic visits away from the office. These visits can refresh as well as inform. In this age of government by committee, you will have to attend at committees in your own department as secretary or member or assessor or chairman, at inter-departmental committees or at an outside body's committee as your department's representative. An ability to speak intelligibly, briefly and cogently is needed in the Home Civil Service just as much as in the Foreign Service. The opportunities for travel tend to grow, even in social service departments; for we are all internationally minded now.[14]

---

14.   Quoted in Richard A. Chapman, *The Higher Civil Service in Britain* (London: Constable, 1970), p. 60.

Chapter Three

Civil Service Grades and the Coordination of Activities

There are several ways of categorising civil servants. When writing of a service which has about 1,000 grades in a total membership of about 47,000, it is desirable to categorise broadly; otherwise there will be a danger of getting lost in a maze of detail. In broad terms, it is generally acceptable to divide the service into two categories: the clerical, executive and administrative classes, and what are generally known as the technical and professional classes.

The former category comprises the general service grades and ranges from clerical assistant, through principal, to secretary of a department. The second category ranges from trainee technician through to the chief technical officer of a department, such as the chief medical officer in the Department of Health or the engineer-in-chief in the Department of Posts and Telegraphs. In addition, there are specialised departmental grades, such as tax officers, which do not fall into either category.

The Devlin report summarises the position in the following paragraphs:

As a general picture, therefore, the civil service consists, first of all, of a central corps of general service officers who are recruited to perform the general duties of Departments from the routine clerical operations to the highest policy advisory and managerial work. These officers are recruited at varying educational levels from primary school leaving to honours university degree standard. The emphasis is on a general education and every recruit can, if he obtains the necessary educational qualifications and experience, aspire to the highest positions in the civil service. . . .
There are, in addition, two groups of specialist classes. The first group consists of those officers who, like general service

officers, are recruited with a general educational qualification, but are assigned to work special to a Department or to a branch of a Department. By intensive on-the-job training, these officers become specialists in their own fields. Examples are the Taxes, Customs and Excise and Estate Duty classes in the Office of the Revenue Commissioners, the Departmental classes in the Post Office and the Social Welfare inspectorate. . . .

The second group of specialist officers are those who are re-cruited to the civil service for the performance of specialised work with a qualification related to the work to be performed. If the qualification is of university degree standard, they are called professional officers; if it is lower, they are called tech-nical officers. As well as the horizontal division between tech-nical and professional officers, there is also a vertical division between different specialities. Engineers, lawyers and doctors, for example, form completely self-contained classes within Departments.[1]

Summarising the position, the report says:

The superficial picture is of a civil service consisting of a general service core grouped around Ministers with an outer layer of Departmental and professional and technical officers to do the executive and consultative work. The actual position of the gen-eral service is somewhat more complicated.

Much of the confusion comes from the role of the Executive grades. In the pre-1920 British civil service, there were no Executive grades. At the centre and grouped around Ministers were the members of the Administrative class, recruited at honours University degree level. These were the Ministerial advisers, the formulators of policy and the general managers of the civil service. They were assisted by members of the clerical grades. . . . Clerical duties ranged from the purely routine to the higher clerical work such as accounts branch work and the

---

1. *Report of Public Services Organisation Review Group 1966–69* (Dublin: Stationery Office, 1969), Prl. 792, pars. 7.4.4 – 7.4.6.

simpler case work bordering on the work of the administrative grades. The normal executive type work of the modern civil service Department did not exist to anything like the same extent that it does today. . . . The 1920 Reorganisation Committee reshaped the general service to provide for an Administrative Class to deal with policy and the general management of the civil service, and a Clerical Class to deal with the routine clerical work. In between, they created an Executive Class to deal with 'the higher work of Supply and Accounting Departments and of other executive or specialised branches of the civil service'. This structure was more or less taken over by the new Irish civil service except that no serious attempt seems to have been made to distinguish between the work of Administrative and Executive staff above the levels of Administrative Officer/Higher Executive Officer. As a result, that work which in Britain was segregated as administrative work is performed here at the higher levels by officers recruited either as Administrative or as Executive Officers. . . . With the assumption of new roles by government, the range of this type of executive work has increased. . . .[2]

The General Service Grades
Commenting on the work of civil servants in the general service, the Devlin report says:

The work of the general service may, therefore, be broken into its main constituents.
  (i) At the higher levels it is concerned with the formulation of policy and preparation of legislation and with the offering of alternative lines to Ministers; it also supplies the secretariat which serves Ministers in a staff capacity.
  (ii) It is concerned with the general management of the civil service. It deals with all personnel, organisation and accounting work in Departments.
  (iii) It deals with blocks of executive type work. . . .
  (iv) It deals with the processing of much of the administrative work of technical branches of the service.[3]

2. ibid., pars. 7.5.1 – 7.5.2.
3. ibid., par. 7.5.3.

The general service grades who perform the work outlined above comprise what are known as higher civil servants (i.e. those in the grades from assistant principal upwards) and those in the executive and clerical grades. Examples of the type of work performed by the higher civil service have been set forth in the preceding chapter. Examples of the work of those in the other general service grades will follow later in this chapter.

The Professional and Technical Grades
The Devlin report has this to say about the departmental and professional and technical classes:

The Departmental and professional and technical grades . . . are employed on specialised technical work either as operators or advisers and are not given general service grading. Some of these specialist staff will be doing quite simple work, e.g., postmen, while at the higher levels many will be doing work with a largely administrative content. . . . Specialist staff are employed in separate structures from the general service staff and their organisation is directly related to their function.[4]

Specialists are of two kinds—those recruited with a general education and trained on the job for a particular function, and those recruited with the formal qualification which they require for the performance of the job. Both types are recruited for particular departments. For example, customs and excise officers are recruited for the Office of the Revenue Commissioners and doctors for the Department of Health.

The professional and technical staff differ from the departmental staff in that their qualification (a university degree or the qualification of a college of technology) is normally conferred by a body outside the civil service and is a marketable commodity in other employments. The expertise of the departmental staff is peculiar to the civil service and is, therefore, imparted within the civil service. For example, the qualifications of an officer of customs and excise are not normally marketable outside the service:

---

4. ibid., par. 7.6.1.

While the distinction between officers regarded as professional and those regarded as technical is related to the source of their qualifications, the drawing of the line is sometimes vague but, once drawn, its consequences are far-reaching. In all professional structures in the civil service there is a rigid barrier beyond which the technical man cannot advance unless he is able to obtain professional qualifications.[5]

Departmental grades are to be found mainly in the Department of Posts and Telegraphs (post office clerks and telephonists) and in the Office of the Revenue Commissioners (inspectors of taxes and customs and excise officers).

There are small groups of departmental grades in other departments also: the social welfare officers in the Department of Social Welfare, and many grades in the Department of Foreign Affairs, such as third secretary and counsellor. The offices of the Houses of the Oireachtas and of the Comptroller and Auditor General also have departmental staffing. In all, the departmental grades comprise rather more than half the total civil service.

Professional and technical officers are to be found in practically all departments. While some, like the Department of the Public Service, employ only a few, others, such as the Department of Agriculture and Fisheries, have more than half of their staff in the professional and technical grades.

To quote again from the Devlin report:

The role of the professional and technical grades is threefold. The first and perhaps the oldest role of the professional officer is to give specialist advice. As the State moved deeper into national life and as the organisation of society became more complex, many policy decisions came to require technical advice. For major issues, the device of a Commission with specialist membership provided the necessary technical input but, for day-to-day questions, it was found necessary to retain specialists within Departments or to engage outside consultants. . . . A second role for the professional officer is to inspect the work of

---

5. ibid., par. 7.6.5.

others and to offer them advice and counsel. This role was. an essential feature of the old local government system when specialist engineering and medical skills were thin on the ground at the local level and were inspected and supplemented by a central cadre with the appropriate skills. While there has been a great increase in expertise at local levels, this role still remains for some specialist staff in the Department of Local Government. The same role can also be seen in some of the technical functions in the Departments of Agriculture and Education. Finally, the third and growing role of the specialist is in the purely executive type operation. With the growth of technology, an increasing number of the executive activities of government are largely technical. Some, such as electricity production, have been hived off to state-sponsored bodies and a number of professional civil service organisations have advocated a similar course for activities within the civil service. Within the civil service, this type of operation includes the Arterial Drainage Section and the Marine Works Section of the Office of Public Works and the Land Project of the Department of Agriculture. Other functions with a technical orientation include the Forestry Division of the Department of Lands which, however, has important commercial and social aspects.[6]

The report notes that:

The role of Departmental grades is, in all cases, to carry out an executive function of government; under the Chief Inspector of Taxes, the Taxes Departmental grades administer the Income Tax code; the Social Welfare Inspectorate is the field force which examines entitlement to social welfare benefits. The broad lines of policy and often the interpretations of cases bearing on policy are handed down from the general service sides of Departments.[7]

Chapter 7 of the report, entitled "The General Organisation of the Civil Service", provides much greater detail on the grading system

---

6.   ibid., par. 7.6.8.
7.   ibid., par. 7.6.4.

in the civil service than it has been considered necessary to set forth here.

The Executive Grades

Executive officers normally work under the supervision of higher executive officers. The duties of the executive officer grade include presenting all the important facts of complicated cases in a readable and logical sequence, summarising accurately the particular issues, recommending a course of action where there are a number of options, drafting briefs for meetings and replies to correspondence, analysing statistical material and accounting for unusual developments.

For example, an executive officer in the Department of Education might be responsible for examining proposals from a school manager or a public body about new or improved school accommodation. This entails finding out the particular needs of an area, taking into account population trends, possible amalgamation of small schools and any special requirements, as well as obtaining reports from professional staff and making recommendations.

An executive officer in the Department of Transport and Power might be responsible for the examination of an application for state assistance for harbour improvement works, having regard to fishing and trade forecasts, revenue forecasts and technical problems (in the light of reports by the technical officers) and for the preparation of a memorandum of conclusions. Drafting work would include such duties as preparing (i) letters to the public and to public representatives, where interpretation of legislation, regulations or policy is concerned, (ii) first drafts of explanatory leaflets and booklets, or (iii) first drafts of memoranda and briefs for departmental or inter-departmental committees or for meetings of international organisations.

Usually the duties of the higher executive grade are partly of a managerial nature and partly administrative. On the managerial side, a higher executive officer directs and controls the work of a number of lower grades and in some cases also coordinates work with technical grades. He is responsible for the training and development of his staff, for their performance and for the achievement of targets within specified time limits.

His administrative duties are an extension of those of the executive officer but at a higher level. A higher executive officer has more responsibility, has to make more difficult decisions, and gives directions where there are exceptions to standard procedures. He is required to initiate work and to organise and review procedures and methods. He assists in the analysis and research for the formulation of policy, in the preparatory work for new legislation, and is responsible for the implementation of policy decisions.

Many specialised jobs are filled by higher executive officers, such as organisation and methods officer, systems analyst and training officer. Nearly all the private secretaries to ministers and to parliamentary secretaries come from this grade. The executive grades in Britain have been referred to as "the solid work horses of every Government Department . . . the most vital [grades] for the smooth functioning of Whitehall."[8]

The Clerical Grades

The duties of clerical assistants include filing papers, recording information, operating office machines, compiling basic statistics, writing cheques and assisting in the paying out of wages, reconciling and balancing uncomplicated accounts in accordance with defined procedures, making and checking arithmetical calculations, checking and analysing documents, accounts and claims, drafting letters and memoranda which follow well-established practice and which seek or give factual information.

Clerical officers allocate, supervise and check the work of clerical assistants and deal with the less straightforward aspects of the work carried out by the lower grade: they make the more complex calculations, raise queries on claims and deal with work which requires substantial dependence on acquired knowledge and experience.

A chart showing the hierarchical structure of the general service grades is at appendix 2. It shows a typical professional/technical structure, as well as the structure in the departmental grade of tax officer in the Office of the Revenue Commissioners.

Coordination

The Devlin report identified the main coordinating systems of the

---

8.   *The Economist*, 26 July 1975, p. 25.

public service as those of planning, finance, personnel and organisation. These are the common functions running through all the separate parts of the service to produce a unity of purpose out of a
diversity of effort.[9]

The report briefly discussed planning as a national activity, as
a background to its consideration of the resources of the civil service
in that area:

> Simply to define planning, we may say that it is the determina-
> tion of the means by which we proceed from a present situation
> to a predetermined goal at a specified future date. Where the
> public business is concerned, the determination of national ob-
> jectives is, in the first place, a political decision and, in the last
> analysis, the choice of ends indicated by the planning process is,
> in a democracy, the prerogative of government. Subject to this,
> the purpose of the planning process is, with agreed goals, to
> seek out, investigate, and evaluate the possible courses of action
> leading to the national goals. Planning must also review progress
> in the implementation of the chosen courses and must contin-
> ually revise these courses in the light of performance and of
> what remains to be performed. At the same time the planning
> process may reveal that goals are either deficient, mutually in-
> compatible or require disproportionate effort for achievement.
> Planning, therefore, will influence the determination of future
> policies.[10]

Planning in the civil service is carried out at two levels, the
micro and the macro. At the micro level, it is performed by the
individual departments, most of which have planning sections. At the
macro level, planning is concerned with the nation as a whole, and
the task of coordinating the various plans of individual departments
and the national plan is done by the Department of Finance which
is the chief source of economic advice to the government. Finance
acts as a coordinating system by virtue of the arrangement under
which departments must obtain the authority of the Department of
Finance before engaging in any activity necessitating new expenditure.

9. ibid., par. 12.4.1.
10. ibid., par. 9.1.1.

Peter Pyne notes that "Since the late nineteen fifties [the Department of Finance] has become the key department primarily responsible for the formulation and coordination of economic policy and planning."[11] A former secretary of that department has written:

> The Finance attitude to proposals involving increased expenditure must inevitably be conditioned not only by the merits of the proposals themselves—not always as apparent to others as to the sponsors—but also by their implications, in conjunction with everything else, for the national finances and the national economy. The first principle of financial administration is the inevitability of choice between competing ends. Nothing new can be undertaken except at the expense of some other possibility. Resources are not inexhaustible; there are, however, no limits to desires. There is no end to the number of things that can be said to be in the national interest. . . .
> Being at the centre, we have to cope with the wants not of one Department but of all and our function is not to select the most meritorious and clap these on the taxpayer's back but, rather, to see that as few as possible emerge as new burdens on the community. There is good reason for this attitude. State expenditure can be met only from taxation or borrowing and in either case is at the expense of the resources available to the community for other purposes.[12]

Coordination of matters in relation to the personnel function is exercised by the Department of the Public Service. While each department has its own personnel division which deals with all matters relating to its own staff (save their recruitment, which is a function of the Civil Service Commission), the general rules are prescribed by the Department of the Public Service. This system ensures that all civil servants, no matter in what department they are employed, are treated alike in their conditions of service. For example, the conditions of eligibility for promotion, the circumstances in which special leave may be allowed, and the rates of expenses payable for travelling on official business, are prescribed by the Department of

11.   Peter Pyne, "The Irish Civil Service", *Administration*, XXII, 1 (1974), 28.
12.   T.K. Whitaker, "The Finance Attitude", *Administration*, II, 3 (1954), 63–64.

the Public Service and apply equally to all departments. At the same time, however, personnel divisions are permitted—indeed encouraged—to administer the regulations with flexibility, having regard to the special circumstances which may arise from situation to situation.

Traditionally, and up to the recent past, matters of organisation were dealt with by the personnel divisions of departments and coordinated by the personnel division of the Department of Finance. However, since the establishment of the Department of the Public Service in 1973, which has separate divisions for personnel and organisation, other departments are being pressed to set up their own organisation divisions and some have done so. These new divisions are concerned with structures: that is to say the organisational framework within which particular tasks are carried out and the grading of the staff assigned to these tasks. The divisions are also concerned with techniques for improving efficiency, known collectively as management services, and with introducing or furthering the use of these in their own departments. The most significant of these services are, perhaps, automatic data processing, cost/utility analysis, management by objectives, systems analysis and design, management accounting systems, and organisation and methods. The organisation divisions in the departments consult and cooperate with the organisation division in the Department of the Public Service.

The personnel and organisation officers of the various departments meet regularly, under the chairmanship of the appropriate deputy secretary of the Department of the Public Service, to discuss specific issues and to exchange views and experiences.

Coordination is achieved in different ways within each department. The four systems already mentioned clearly have a coordinating role. For example, the personnel division coordinates matters relating to the staffing of the department, while the accounts or finance division regulates financial matters.

With regard to the various tasks which fall to be performed by the individual departments, R.G.S. Brown writes:

The work of government departments can be broken down into a large number of more or less self-contained tasks which have to be coordinated. In isolation each task presents its own technical problems calling for special knowledge and techniques in anything from office management to operational research. But each task also has to be related to others. If it is instrumental to some broad aim of policy it has to be controlled and kept under review, so that the means does not become an end in itself. Primary coordination is normally achieved by grouping tasks in departments.[13]

He goes on:

A Minister usually sees a sample of the work carried out in different parts of his department. His mind is likely to fasten on common elements, if only because considerations that came up in connection with problem A are still at the back of his mind a few minutes later when he looks at problem B from the other 'side' of his department. If he feels that an important connection is being missed, he has the authority to ask for a review. . . . What goes for the Minister also goes for senior advisers and administrators who prepare material for his decision and take decisions on his behalf.[14]

Inter-departmental committees coordinate in cases where a number of departments have an interest in a particular subject. These are committees comprised of officials of the departments concerned. Examples of such committees, further to those indicated in the previous chapter, are those on the environment, on the coordination of the negotiations leading to Ireland's membership of the European Community, or on the problems of small western farms, under the auspices of the Departments of Local Government, Foreign Affairs, and Agriculture and Fisheries, respectively.

Referring to the question of general policy coordination, the Devlin committee made a specific recommendation in relation to the role of the Department of the Taoiseach:

In its Cabinet Office role, the main task of the Department is the coordination of Government business. At present there is a tendency for the plans of individual Departments which impinge on the activities of others to have reached an advanced stage

13.   Op. cit., p. 197.
14.   ibid., pp. 202–03.

before these other Departments are consulted. Furthermore, there are issues not the responsibility of any Minister which, under the Ministers and Secretaries Acts, devolve on the Taoiseach. We recommend that the Cabinet Office side of the Taoiseach's Department should attend to these matters. Once any decision is taken by a Minister to initiate studies which will concern more than one Department, that decision should be communicated to the Taoiseach's Department which should nominate one of its own staff, or request the lead Department concerned to nominate one of its staff, to chair a committee to be responsible for pursuing the matter and bringing it to the stage where it is ready for Ministerial decision.[15]

In the context of coordination, it is reasonable to mention also the informal contacts which are constantly taking place between civil servants at all levels, on social occasions, at meetings, and at training courses.

---

15. Op. cit., par. 15.6.3.

Chapter Four

A Particular Example: the Department of Agriculture and Fisheries

Since the author has been a civil servant for many years in the Department of Agriculture and Fisheries and is familiar with its activities, this chapter describes in some detail the Department's work, as an illustration of the kind of tasks undertaken by Irish civil servants.

The Department of Agriculture and Fisheries is the oldest of the existing departments of state, dating from 1900 when it was established as the Department of Agriculture and Technical Instruction for Ireland. In addition to being one of the larger departments, it is regarded as one of the most important in view of the significance of agriculture to the Irish economy. In 1974 agriculture accounted for about 16 per cent. of the gross national product, for the employment of over 23 per cent. of the total labour force and for 35 per cent. of the country's total exports. As well as providing employment in primary production on farms and in the manufacture of farm inputs (such as fertilisers and feeding stuffs), agriculture provides the basic raw materials for many more of the country's important industries, including meat and milk processing, sugar and flour production, brewing and distilling. National growth depends very heavily on Ireland's capacity to develop its agricultural industry which contributes so much to the export trade. The estimated exchequer expenditure on agriculture in 1976 is £114.36m. while an additional £2.8m., derived from local rates, is expected to be spent by the county committees of agriculture. The expenditure on fisheries is expected to be £8.09m.

Aims and Objectives

The aims of the department are to promote the economic progress of agriculture and the social progress of the agricultural population

44

and to increase the agricultural sector's contribution to the economy as a whole. Although the contribution to the economy of the fisheries sector is far less than that of agriculture, its value, including its amenity value, is appreciable.

The last formal published statement of the objectives of Irish agricultural policy was contained in the Third Programme for Economic and Social Development 1969–72. The stated objectives were: increasing efficiency in the production, processing and marketing of farm products; ensuring that agriculture makes the highest possible contribution to the economic and social progress of the nation; ensuring that farmers who work their land fully and efficiently share equitably in the growing national prosperity and that a reasonable relationship is maintained between farm incomes and incomes in other occupations; improving the structure of agriculture and strengthening the economic and competitive capacity of the viable family farm; aiding the smaller and economically more vulnerable farmer to secure an acceptable level of income; improving the conditions of access to external markets for agricultural exports.[1] The programme went on to say that these objectives were interdependent and, together, were designed to maintain the maximum number of people on the land consistent with social and economic progress.

Since that programme was prepared, Ireland has become a member of the European Community. The objectives of the Community's common agricultural policy, as laid down in the Treaty of Rome, are:

(a) to increase agricultural productivity by promoting technical progress and by ensuring the rational development of agricultural production and the optimum utilisation of the factors of production, in particular labour;

(b) thus to ensure a fair standard of living for the agricultural community, in particular by increasing the individual earnings of persons engaged in agriculture;

(c) to stabilise markets;

(d) to assure the availability of supplies;

---

1. *Third Programme. Economic and Social Development 1969–72* (Dublin: Stationery Office, 1969), Prl. 431, chapter 5.

(e) to ensure that supplies reach consumers at reasonable prices.[2]

   The main organ for carrying out the government's agricultural policy is the Department of Agriculture and Fisheries. It does this through the provision of education and advice; the formulation and administration of schemes to improve farmland, buildings and facilities; the operation of measures to improve livestock and crop production and to eliminate and control disease; the operation of measures to ensure high standards in agricultural processing and marketing; and the negotiation of improved access to export markets. The department itself, and bodies associated with it, carry out inquiries, experiments and research on agricultural and fishery matters. They also collect and publish information.
   The department's activities vitally affect both the agricultural and fishing industries. While it does not itself directly engage—except incidentally to other work—in the economic activities of these industries, it can properly be regarded as forming part of them. The agricultural industry embraces more than farming. It extends far beyond the farm gate into processing and marketing, and the work of the department reflects this; the outcome of European Community deliberations, in which it continuously participates, has a major influence on the industry. The various ways in which state or EEC monies are expended, and the amounts made available, affect the direction and progress of the industry. The same holds true for fisheries. There are, of course, influencing factors, such as market and weather conditions, over which the department can exercise little or no control.
   The services within the department include the personnel and organisation functions, while on the financial side there is the considerable task of making payments and monitoring expenditure, estimated at £122.4m. in 1976. Financial requirements for the coming year have to be estimated and forecasts must be made of expenditure for several years ahead. Closely linked with this is a scrutiny of the return which expenditure is yielding or is likely to yield. This entails examining how the agricultural and fishing industries have per-

---

2. *Treaty Establishing the European Economic Community and connected documents* (Brussels: European Communities, 1958), Article 39.

formed in the past, how they are currently faring, and what the proposals are for future years. Data on expenditure have to be linked with economic data. It is not easy to gauge what the economic effects of expenditure are. However, a good groundwork for deeper analysis is laid by a systematic grouping of activities into what are called programmes, by reference to their objectives, by calculating the expenditure on each of the programmes and by measuring— mainly in economic terms—progress towards the achievement of objectives.

The total staff employed by the department is about 4,400.[3] Roughly one-third are in the general service grades and a similar proportion work at headquarters in Dublin; the remainder work from various locations in the country. The department has about ninety local offices in country towns, and many of its schemes are administered from these centres. In addition to its local offices, the department runs four agricultural colleges with large farms attached; a central veterinary laboratory with a number of regional laboratories; the National Butter Testing Station and regional dairying laboratories; progeny and performance test stations for cattle and pigs; and a number of other institutions such as the National Botanic Gardens and the National Seed Testing Station.

From the organisation charts at appendix 3 it will be seen that the activities of the department are carried out by a number of administrative divisions and technical groups. It would be tedious to attempt to set out in detail the work of each of these but, by choosing a few administrative divisions and broadly describing what they do, and by outlining the work of the technical groups, it is hoped that a representative picture will be formed of the type of work carried out by civil servants in this particular department.

Education Division

There are about 36 general service officers in this division. Working in close collaboration with these are the technical staff under the heading "Group A – Committees of Agriculture and Advisory Services", at page 67 of the *Directory of State Services 1976*. The

3. Particulars of the numbers in each of the various grades are contained in the *Directory of State Services 1976* (Dublin: Stationery Office, 1976), Prl. 4889.

division has two branches, one of which deals with the county committees of agriculture and the other with agricultural education.

Each county has a committee of agriculture which is established and operates under legislation. The purpose of the committees is to operate a range of agricultural schemes (mainly advisory) designed to develop agriculture and to benefit rural-dwellers. Each committee employs a staff of instructors in agriculture, in horticulture, in poultry-keeping and in farm home-management. The qualifications, salaries, conditions of service and range of duties of these instructors are prescribed by the department, which maintains a statutory control over them and over the entire range of activities of the committees. The department contributes somewhat more than half of the total cost of the committees' expenditure, and schemes operated by the committees must be approved in advance by the department through its education division.

The educational activities of the department fall under three heads: education for young men, for young women, and grants to universities. Young men who have completed their general education can undertake a comprehensive one-year course based on a standard syllabus, including all aspects of agriculture, which is provided in eleven agricultural colleges, including the four which are administered directly by the department. Horticultural education is provided at three residential colleges and also at the National Botanic Gardens.

Courses in rural home economics for young women are taught at seven privately owned colleges. In all cases, the department, through its education division, conducts uniform examinations at the end of the course and awards diplomas and certificates.

Advanced three-year residential courses are provided at the state-owned Munster Institute, Cork, for young women who wish to qualify for teaching and advisory posts on poultry-keeping and farm home-management.

The staff engaged in the state-owned colleges are employed by the department. The staff in the privately owned colleges are employed directly by the colleges but the department contributes towards the cost of their salaries, ensures that they are appropriately qualified, that the teaching is of a high standard and is conducted on broadly similar lines at all seven institutions.

Higher education in general agriculture and in horticulture, leading to university degrees, is provided by University College, Dublin. University College, Cork offers a degree course in dairy science. Education in veterinary medicine and surgery, leading to university degrees, is provided by both Dublin universities. The department pays annual grants to all these colleges after examining their submitted proposals. In 1976 these grants are estimated at about £3.7m.

A white paper, outlining the views of the government on the reorganisation of the existing agricultural education, advisory and research services, was published in 1975.[4] This document records the government's decision to amalgamate these services under a separate authority, to be constituted as an executive agency of the Minister for Agriculture and Fisheries on the lines indicated in the Devlin report. Legislation to implement this decision is being prepared at the time of writing.

Livestock Breeding Division
The purpose of this division is the improvement of livestock. The importance of livestock in the Irish economy hardly needs to be stated. In 1974 livestock output accounted for nearly 55 per cent. of the gross agricultural output; livestock and livestock products together accounted for 84 per cent. of the agricultural output. Of Ireland's total domestic exports, 32 per cent. consisted of exports of livestock and livestock products. The great bulk of these exports consisted of cattle and sheep and products deriving from these animals.

As in the education division, officers of the technical staff collaborate with the general service officers. The work of the division is divided into three broad heads: cattle, pigs and sheep. Until recently, executive duties relating to horse breeding were also dealt with in the division but these were transferred to Bord na gCapall (Irish Horse Board) in 1975.

The department's policy in relation to cattle involves the licensing of bulls so as to ensure that only animals of a high standard are used for breeding; the licensing of artificial insemination stations; the supervision of purchases of pedigree livestock abroad by private

---

4. *A National Agricultural, Advisory, Education and Research Authority* (Dublin: Stationery Office, 1975), Prl. 4501.

interests, including the import of some pedigree bulls for leasing to breeders; recording the milk yields of pedigree cows and other lesser schemes.

The improvement schemes for pigs and sheep are broadly on the same lines as those for cattle.

A number of state-sponsored bodies—Bord na gCon (Irish Greyhound Board), Bord na gCapall, An Chomhairle Olla (The Wool Council) and the National Stud—come under the aegis of the livestock division. The division is responsible for ensuring that the bodies comply with all the provisions of the statutes governing their establishment and operation: the arrangements for the nomination of members; the remuneration of staff; the preparation of expenditure estimates; the presentation to the Dáil of annual reports and accounts; the preparation of amending legislation when required; the formulation of replies to parliamentary questions, and such various other matters as may arise in relation to the minister's responsibilities for the activities of the boards. To this end, the officers of the livestock division maintain a close and friendly relationship with their public service colleagues in these bodies.

European Community Affairs

There are several divisions dealing with various aspects of Ireland's membership of the European Community. One of these is concerned with the policy formulation and negotiating processes of the Community's trade links with individual countries and with regional groupings of countries, a network that covers most of the world. Activities in the field of trade at the time of writing include participation in the multilateral trade negotiations—the so-called Tokyo round—being conducted under the aegis of the General Agreement on Tariffs and Trade (GATT) and involving more than a hundred countries; the development of the Community's links with the countries of the Mediterranean basin; and the implementation of the Lomé Convention, an association agreement with the developing countries of the African, Caribbean and Pacific regions.

These wide-ranging activities require a correspondingly extensive knowledge of the trading patterns and potential of the Community's trade partners. They involve considerable study of tariff schedules and preferential trading arrangements, as well as analysis and assessment of proposed concessions to determine their probable effect on Ireland's trading interests. They also demand a great deal of travelling to attend meetings of the EEC foreign trade institutions and meetings between the Community and its trading partners.

Ireland is now an integral part of the world's largest trading bloc. Within the Community she has a legitimate right and duty to protect and foster her trading interests. At the same time she is required to keep her sights focussed on the world at large, to promote the trading interests of the Community as a whole, and to help to meet those obligations and responsibilities to both developed and underdeveloped countries which her size and influence impose.

Another division is, under the European Communities Act 1972, responsible for the operation of the Community mechanisms in relation to market support for beef. These include the intervention system, which is designed to support market prices. The department is the official intervention agency and is therefore responsible for the operation of the support systems.

Market intervention is a new and unusual feature of the activities of a government department, since it involves the direct participation by the department in commercial activities. These activities include the inspection, grading and purchase of the beef offered for intervention, supervision of deboning operations, control of freezing, transport and storage and the eventual sale of the product. The funds for the purchase of the beef are provided by the national exchequer and any losses on sales are subsequently reimbursed by FEOGA (the European Agricultural Guidance and Guarantee Fund).

The scale of the work involved in beef intervention may be judged from the magnitude of the purchases: 2,300 tonnes in 1973, 120,000 tonnes in 1974 and 135,000 tonnes in 1975. The amounts purchased in 1974 and 1975 represented over 40 per cent. and 35 per cent. respectively of total cattle slaughterings for export in those years. The amount of national funds involved in stocks of intervention beef has reached levels of over £100 million.

The staff who deal with Community affairs spend a considerable proportion of their time servicing meetings in Brussels. This is very demanding.

Fisheries Division

This division is divided into two more or less self-contained areas—sea fisheries and inland fisheries. The staff is divided equally into general service officers and technical officers; the latter include scientists and engineers in various grades.

The sea fisheries section is responsible for the administration of sea fishery legislation: size limits for fish, close seasons, infringement of exclusive fishery limits; the operation of schemes for training fishermen, including the running of a fisheries school at Greencastle, County Donegal; scientific investigations and research on sea-fish, including the operation of exploratory fishing vessels; the regulation of fish imports; the development of five harbours as major fishery harbour centres, two of which are under the direct management of the department; trade in fishery products; the setting of standards for exports of processed products; market investigations; and the control and eradication of marine pollution.

The inland fisheries section deals with matters relating to salmon, trout and coarse fishing, sea-angling and eel-fishing, and with the bodies responsible for the protection and development of such fisheries, including the Boards of Fishery Conservators. Of the existing local authorities, these boards are the oldest, dating back to 1848. They are charged under statute with the conservation of fisheries within their districts and are composed in the main of members elected by holders of fishing licences and fishery owners who are empowered, *inter alia*, to levy rates on the fisheries in their districts. By employing waterkeepers, they arrange for the fisheries to be protected. The boards operate under the guidance and control of the department.

The inland section also prepares legislation and by-laws for the protection of fish stocks, including the prevention of pollution; undertakes scientific investigation and experiments; promotes schemes for the improvement of salmon fisheries and the development of fish farming and eel-fishing; arranges for the management and letting of over a hundred state-owned fisheries; and supervises the fisheries functions exercised by the Electricity Supply Board on the rivers Shannon, Erne, Lee and Liffey. At the time of writing, the division is examining the comprehensive report of the Inland Fisheries Commission, published in 1975, on all facets of inland fisheries.[5] The report embodies some two-hundred recommendations, many of which are of a far-reaching nature, suggesting changes in existing structures and requiring legislation to implement them.

In all of the foregoing activities, officers in the general service and in the technical grades collaborate closely.

Under the aegis of the fisheries division fall two state-sponsored bodies: Bord Iascaigh Mhara (Sea Fisheries Board) and the Inland Fisheries Trust. The division's responsibilities for, and liaison with, these bodies are similar to those outlined above in relation to the livestock division and its associated organisations. Senior officers of the division are members of the board in each case.

Other organisations with which the division has a direct link, and which are financed in part by the department, are the Foyle Fisheries Commission and the Salmon Research Trust. The Commission, established under statute in 1952, is an inter-governmental agency which has responsibility for conserving, protecting and improving the fisheries of the river Foyle and its tributaries on both sides of the Northern Ireland/Republic of Ireland border. Two officers of the fisheries division are members of the Commission, the chairmanship of which rotates annually between the senior officer in the north and his counterpart in the south.

The Salmon Research Trust operates under the joint auspices of the Minister for Agriculture and Fisheries and Messrs. Arthur Guinness Son and Company Limited; its members include two representatives of the minister, who are normally officers of the fisheries division.

The Farm Development Service
Directives adopted by the European Community have the force of law in each member country. In Ireland, the farm modernisation scheme was introduced early in 1974 to give effect to Directive 159 which has two broad objectives: firstly, by means of a selective system of aids, to encourage the development of as many farms as possible capable of giving the farmer a fair income and living conditions at least as good as the non-farm worker and, secondly, to

---

5. *Report of the Inland Fisheries Commission* (Dublin: Stationery Office, 1975), Prl. 4712.

harmonise the levels and types of these aids throughout the Community. The scheme, of necessity, follows the directive to the letter. It is also a comprehensive scheme embracing all the aids towards capital investment open to farmers and, as such, replaces a number of capital grant schemes previously operated by the department. The scheme emphasises the importance of farm planning.

Administration is divided between the local agricultural advisory services, operated by the twenty-seven county committees of agriculture, and the department's farm development service which has a central unit in Dublin and some seventy local offices. The farmer applies to the head of the county advisory service, who decides on the applicant's classification under the scheme, which in turn determines the category of aid to which he is entitled. After consultation between the farmer and his agricultural adviser, the farm plan is prepared. This normally provides for the carrying out of a variety of works—buildings, drainage, fencing and the installation of water and equipment. The local office of the farm development service then administers the grants for these works. This requires on-site inspections of the farm, preparation of plans and specifications, laying down special conditions (for example, in regard to pollution control), inspection on completion to see that the conditions are met, and finally certifying to head office for payment. Because of the nature of the work, the staff of local offices of the service are mainly technical officers. However, they are backed up by clerical assistants who carry out the regular jobs that arise in every office—filing, keeping records, compiling statistics, and so on.

The work of the farm development service at headquarters, on the other hand, involves much more than paying out grants to farmers. For one thing, part of the exchequer cost for one particular category of farmer, the 'development' farmer, is recoverable from Community funds. This requires the maintenance of very detailed records to meet EEC requirements and in order to be able to lodge prompt and accurate claims for recoupment. Besides, the Community's farm structure policy is not static, and ideas for change, and improvements to it, are constantly under examination. For these reasons, the farm development service unit in Dublin comprises a team of administrative and technical officers dealing with both the modernisation scheme itself and general policy issues.

Since the scheme affects every farmer, it attracts a large volume of correspondence from farmers themselves and from public representatives writing on their behalf. Draft edicts or other documents issued from Brussels must be scrutinised, summarised and their implications examined. Meetings, with farm organisations wishing to propose changes in the scheme, with manufacturers' associations concerned about the trends of demand from farmers, or with credit institutions seeking to explore credit demands, are regular features of the civil servant's work. Meetings in Brussels of standing committees or *ad hoc* working groups, or for bilateral discussions with the Commission, must also be attended. There is regular contact by telephone or correspondence with the chief agricultural officers around the country, in order to solve administrative and other problems by mutual consultation. There is regular monitoring of the progress of the scheme, analysis of expenditure and other statistical data, and forecasting of future trends.

The Agricultural Inspectorate

The agricultural inspectorate collaborates with the general service grades in nearly all aspects of the department's activities. The duties of the inspectorate, which is headed by a chief inspector, are broken down into seven broad categories: advisory, livestock, cereals and plant-breeding, dairy produce, potatoes and feeding stuffs, agricultural education and poultry and eggs, and horticulture. Very briefly the work involved in each of these areas is as follows.

Advisory: Provision of assistance to the committees of agriculture in drawing up their annual financial estimates; in providing in-service training for the local staffs; in formulating effective county programmes and securing their implementation; and in providing liaison on general agricultural matters between the department and the committees, as well as giving specialist advice.

Livestock: The inspectorate is closely involved in the formulation and execution of the various plans and programmes for the improvement of livestock.

Cereals and Plant Breeding: The breeding, selection, propagation and testing of new cereal varieties (wheat, oats, barley), the testing of varieties of other crops and the production of certified seed; the implementation of EEC directives on seed; seed testing and seed control.

Dairy Products: Administration of the legislation relating to the manufacture of dairy products. This involves the inspection of all the activities carried out at creameries and at premises for the manufacture of cheese, chocolate crumb and condensed milk; the checking and verification of milk weights and butter fat tests; the chemical and bacteriological analysis of butter.

Potatoes and Feeding Stuffs: Administration of the national seed potato certification scheme to ensure disease-free seed and pure stock. Inspection of the manufacture of feeding stuffs, fertilisers and mineral mixtures and the drawing of samples for analysis; the operation of the plant health service; duties relating to flour milling, the import of cereals, inspection at mills and facilities for drying and storing grain.

Agricultural Education, Poultry and Eggs: Supervision of the courses at the state-owned and state-aided agricultural colleges and the operation of the farms attached to these colleges; poultry education and research; inspection of egg dealers' premises; assistance in the operation of the schemes of the county committees of agriculture.

Horticulture: Advising on policy for the development and expansion of horticulture, including assisting the local horticultural staff in the formulation of effective county programmes; provision of technical advice to co-operative societies engaged in the production and/or marketing of horticultural produce; arrangements for the provision of healthy planting material; measures relating to the control and inspection of imported horticultural produce in order to prevent disease; provision of the two-year courses in amenity horticulture at the National Botanic Gardens and in commercial horticulture at Kildalton College, County Kilkenny.

The Veterinary Inspectorate

The veterinary inspectorate collaborates with the general service staff in the various areas of the department where veterinary matters arise: in the animal health division, the meat division and, to a lesser extent, in the poultry, dairying and livestock divisions. The inspectorate is headed by the director of veterinary services and its duties are divided into three main categories—field work, food hygiene and research.

The field work relates to disease prevention, control and eradication. Prevention duties embrace matters relating to the circumstances in which animals and animal products may be allowed into the country, bearing in mind Ireland's unique freedom from major animal diseases. Eradication duties embrace the national schemes for such diseases as bovine tuberculosis, brucellosis and sheep scab and include the measures which have to be taken in the event of an outbreak of a major disease such as foot and mouth disease, fowl pest or swine fever. Control measures comprise the investigation of disease problems, where formal eradication schemes do not obtain, and various aspects of veterinary education, including lectures and the dissemination of literature.

The food hygiene work relates mainly to the direct supervision of all aspects of the production of meat for export (including fresh meat, bacon and poultry) and to the general supervision, in liaison with local authorities, of meat produced for the home market.

The research work embraces duties in relation to the diagnosis of disease in cattle, sheep, pigs, equines, poultry, fish, fur-bearing animals and bees; tests on animals for import or for export; specific research projects; giving advice when necessary, e.g. on disease-control measures or on the safety of vaccines.

State-Sponsored Bodies

The following state-sponsored bodies are under the aegis of the department: Bord na gCapall, Bord na gCon, Bord Iascaigh Mhara, An Chomhairle Olla, Córas Beostoic agus Feola Teoranta (Irish Livestock and Meat Board), The Dairy Disposal Company Limited, the Dublin and Cork District Milk Boards, An Foras Taluntais (The Agricultural Institute), The Inland Fisheries Trust Incorporated, Irish Potato Marketing, The Irish National Stud Company Limited and the Pigs and Bacon Commission. In addition, during 1976 the department will take over responsibility from the Department of Finance for Comhlucht Siúicre Eireann Teo. (The Irish Sugar Company) and The Racing Board. Each body is 'attached' to a specific division of the department, which exercises the same form of surveillance over it as the livestock division does for the state-sponsored bodies attached to it.

Another body connected with the department is Gorta (The Freedom from Hunger Council of Ireland). Although Gorta is a national organisation, established by the government in 1965 at the request of the Food and Agriculture Organisation of the United Nations to help eradicate hunger and malnutrition in the third world, its members are appointed by the Minister for Agriculture and Fisheries.

Advisory Bodies

One of the recommendations of the report of the British Machinery of Government Committee (the Haldane committee)[6] was that advisory committees should form an integral part of the normal organisation of a department. The Department of Agriculture and Fisheries, in common with most other departments, has attached to it a number of such committees or bodies, established to advise the minister on various matters arising out of his functions. These bodies[7] are comprised in the main of representatives of agricultural interests. For example, the cattle advisory committee advises the minister on all aspects of cattle breeding, including import policy. It includes representatives of eleven organisations, including the Irish Farmers' Association, the National Executive of the Livestock Trade and the Pedigree Cattle Breeders Council.

Another such body is the Animal Remedies Consultative Committee which is provided for in the Animal Remedies Act 1956. It includes representatives of the Veterinary Council, the Pharmaceutical Society of Ireland and the Irish Creamery Milk Suppliers' Association. Its purpose is to advise and assist the minister in making regulations under the Act.

Appellate Bodies

The Department of Agriculture and Fisheries, like some other departments, administers a number of statutes, which confer or deny

---

6. *Ministry of Reconstruction: Report of the Machinery of Government Committee* (London: HMSO, 1918), par. 34.
7. Particulars of the advisory bodies attached to each department are included in the *Administration Yearbook and Diary*, published annually by the Institute of Public Administration, Dublin.

a benefit, or impose or absolve citizens from an obligation. In the case of some of these statutes, the legislature has seen fit to provide facilities for the appeal and review of administrative decisions.The bodies to which appeals may be made are known as administrative tribunals, that is, "a person or body of persons, other than a court of justice, established under statute to adjudicate upon issues arising in the course of administration of that body of legislation, original and delegated, which is termed administrative law." [8]

For example, under Section 3(6)(b) and (d) of the Livestock Marts Act 1967,[9] provision is made for the holding of an inquiry, at the request of a licence holder, in relation to a proposal by the Minister for Agriculture and Fisheries to revoke a licence granted to the licensee to operate a livestock mart. The inquiry in this case must be held by a practising barrister of at least ten-years standing. Like provision is made under Section 29(3)(b)(ii) of the Horse Industry Act 1970[10] for the holding of an inquiry where the minister proposes to revoke a licence to keep a riding establishment. Under two statutes relating to livestock breeding, provision is made for an appeal to a referee against refusal by the department to grant licences in respect of animals intended for breeding.

Provision is also made for an appeal against certain decisions of some of the state-sponsored bodies which are under the aegis of the department. For example, Section 51(1) of the Greyhound Industry Act 1958[11] provides for an appeal to an appeals committee against refusal or suspension by Bord na gCon of licences or permits under the Act.

It is of interest to note that certain directives of the European Community, while not making specific provision for subjecting administrative decisions to scrutiny by, or appeal to, another body, presuppose the existence of facilities for appeal.[12]

8. Vincent Grogan, *Administrative Tribunals in the Public Service* (Dublin: Institute of Public Administration, 1961), p. 9.

9. Livestock Marts Act 1967 (no. 20).

10. Horse Industry Act 1970 (no. 19).

11. Greyhound Industry Act 1958 (no. 12).

12. Directive 74/150/EEC: Article 14 in relation to the harmonisation of legislation dealing with tractors.

Finances

The Department of Agriculture and Fisheries must, like all other departments of state, obtain the authority of the Dáil for the money spent on grants, subsidies, salaries and so on by the department itself, by the local authorities associated with the department (the county committees of agriculture and the boards of fishery conservators), and by the state-sponsored bodies which are attached to the department.

The procedure for obtaining this authorisation is that, several months before the beginning of the financial year, the head of each administrative division is required to submit estimates of the amount of money which, in the following year, the division will spend on, and receive from, the services it provides. These estimates are then coordinated into the department's total estimate which is divided into subheads and subsections of subheads for accounting purposes. Thus, subhead A contains the provision for salaries and subhead B.8 the provision for county committees of agriculture. The estimates are submitted for approval to the secretary of the department who, as accounting officer, is responsible for the regularity and propriety of all financial transactions. The minister's formal approval for the estimate is then obtained, after which it is passed to the Department of Finance. The Department of Finance coordinates all departmental estimates into an overall estimate for government services. This entails balancing the projected expenditure with expected revenue. At this stage there is considerable discussion between the Department of Finance and the other departments, since invariably the amount proposed to be spent is greater than the anticipated revenue.

The estimates are then published in book form and presented to the Dáil which approves them in due course, thus providing the necessary authority for the spending of money. The estimates may be subject to debate before being passed. Since the financial year may have commenced before the estimates are passed, there is a special statutory provision—the Central Fund (Permanent Provisions) Act 1965 [13]—enabling the spending of a proportion of the money before the estimates are actually passed. If during the year it is thought that actual expenditure will exceed the estimate, a supplementary estimate

---

13.   Central Fund (Permanent Provisions) Act 1965 (no. 26).

is prepared, submitted to the Department of Finance and put before the Dáil in the usual way.

At the end of the financial year, an appropriation account is prepared which shows the actual expenditure and receipts (or appropriations in aid, as they are called) during the year, side by side with the amounts in the estimate as approved by the Dáil. Savings and excesses on the various subheads are explained and the account is then audited by the Comptroller and Auditor General. When he is satisfied, he presents his report to the Dáil. The report is then considered by the public accounts committee, a special committee of the Dáil. In the course of its examination of the accounts, the committee calls the accounting officer before it and, having heard his evidence, presents its report with recommendations to the House. An extract from the minutes of a typical meeting of the committee is at appendix 4.

The Minister for Agriculture and Fisheries
Since this book relates to the civil service, and this particular chapter specifically to the work of the civil servants in the Department of Agriculture and Fisheries, it would hardly be appropriate to end the chapter without making at least a brief reference to some of the duties of the minister in charge of that department.

The enormous burden of work placed on a minister of state has been outlined in chapter two. As head of a department, he is, under the Ministers and Secretaries Acts, entirely responsible to Dáil Eireann for all its activities and for the actions of all of its officers, except for matters relating to finance, which are the responsibility of the accounting officer.

With over 200 interest groups concerned with agriculture and fisheries, the minister meets many deputations from members of these groups in the course of his work. The Department of Agriculture and Fisheries has compiled a list of client organisations, including state-sponsored bodies, which from time to time might request meetings with the minister to discuss matters relating to their own particular interest. These organisations may be categorised as follows (the numbers in brackets indicate the number of bodies in each category): general agricultural interests (30); cattle (30); cereals and foodstuffs (10); horses (22); horticulture and bee-keeping (13); milk and dairy products (17); pigs (6); mink (1); poultry (8); sheep and wool (28); fisheries (47).

The biggest of these groups and organisations are the Irish Farmers' Association, the Irish Creamery Milk Suppliers' Association, the Irish Agricultural Organisation Society Limited, the Irish Countrywomen's Association, the Irish Sugar Beet Growers' Association, Macra na Feirme and Muintir na Tíre. Small size does not necessarily mean, however, that an organisation has little influence; for example, the Irish Livestock Exporters' and Traders' Association, which has a relatively small membership, has major influence. It is involved in a key area of the economy, as its title suggests.

Although there is no statutory obligation on a minister to answer parliamentary questions, custom dictates that he does so. In 1974 the Minister for Agriculture and Fisheries or his Parliamentary Secretary answered a total of 735 parliamentary questions in Dáil Eireann. These consisted of 617 questions on agriculture and 118 questions on fishery matters; 577 of the questions on agriculture were answered orally, and the other forty answers were given to the questioning deputies in written form. As regards fishery matters, 114 were oral answers and the remaining four were written. (At present the Minister for Agriculture and Fisheries has a Parliamentary Secretary to whom responsibility in relation to fishery matters is delegated by law and who in fact answers nearly all the questions on that subject.) The range of questions which the minister may be required to answer is very broad. On one particular day he answered twenty-five questions on eighteen different subjects.[14]

Since Ireland's accession to the European Community, much of the minister's time has been spent abroad attending meetings, particularly at Community headquarters in Brussels. This was especially true of the first half of 1975 when, during the period of Ireland's Presidency of the Council of the European Communities, the minister was chairman of the Council of Ministers for Agriculture. During that six-month period he left the country seventeen times to attend official meetings abroad.

---

14. *Dáil Debates*, Vol. 272, No. 4, 1 May 1974, Cols. 486–516.

Chapter Five

Recruitment and Promotion

In the vast majority of cases, civil servants must be selected for appointment by the Civil Service Commission. Such a body has been in existence since 1855, following the recommendations of the Northcote-Trevelyan Report. The Act under which the Commission now operates is the Civil Service Commissioners Act 1956.[1] The Commission consists of three persons who are, at present, the Ceann Comhairle of Dáil Eireann, the Secretary to the government (who is also the Secretary to the Department of the Taoiseach) and the Director of Recruitment in the Department of the Public Service. The Commission has a staff of about 170 civil servants who make the arrangements for the various competitions.

The two main categories of position in the civil service are established and unestablished. The 1956 Act stipulates that appointments to established, or permanent, positions must be made (i) following the holding of a competition by the Civil Service Commission, or (ii) by the government.[2] The services of an established civil servant can be terminated only by the government.

The method of appointment of unestablished civil servants is the same as for established persons. Generally, unestablished personnel are appointed to posts, the long-term necessity for which is not obvious, or where it is deemed desirable that officers being appointed to a particular grade should undergo a trial period in an unestablished capacity before being appointed in an established capacity. The services of an unestablished officer can be terminated by the minister in charge of the department in which the officer is serving.

1. Civil Service Commissioners Act 1956 (no. 45).
2. Section 13.

In cases where the government decides it would be in the public interest that a particular person should be appointed to the civil service, the Civil Service Commission has no function to perform. The procedure is that the minister to whose department the person is to be appointed must first of all obtain the consent of the Minister for the Public Service to the appointment and then must also obtain the government's approval. Such appointments are rare and, when they are made, notice about them must be published in *Iris Oifigiúil*, the official gazette. If any questions are raised in the Dáil or elsewhere about the appointment, the appropriate minister and the government must be prepared to defend it.

Further types of appointment (or perhaps 'reappointment' would be a more accurate term) in which the Civil Service Commission plays a relatively minor part relate to widows, or to women not being supported by their husbands because of either desertion or incapacity, who prior to their leaving the service (at the time when female civil servants had to retire on marriage) were established civil servants. Subject to certain conditions, such women may be re-admitted to the civil service without having to take part in a competition. The reappointment is made by the minister in charge of the department in which they formerly served and is usually in an unestablished capacity for a trial period. Subsequent appointment in an established capacity can only be effected with the concurrence of the Civil Service Commission.

Further exceptions to appointment by the Civil Service Commission relate to certain broad categories of person such as skilled artisans, messengers, cleaners, and casual or part-time employees. The Schedule to the Act states that the Commission's competitive procedures do not apply to these employments, and the manner in which recruitment is effected is therefore left to the individual department. Sometimes an advertisement is inserted in the national or local newspapers; at other times the local office of the Department of Labour is requested to send to the department for interview any persons whose names are on its books and who seem suited to the particular position. Applicants are then interviewed and the general practice is that the name of the successful candidate is submitted to the minister in charge of the department for his approval.

The Civil Service Commission is not concerned with individual appointments made through promotion in the 'customary course', as determined by the commissioners:

> As regards promotion in the customary course, the Commissioners have made determinations that promotions in each of the grade-to-grade progressions in the general service, Departmental and professional hierarchical structures are in the customary course. A promotion outside the customary course, e.g. Executive Officer to Assistant Principal (skipping a grade) or Engineer to Assistant Principal (crossing class barriers) cannot be made except as a result of a competition or until the promotee is accepted by the Commissioners as qualified for the new appointment. Promotion from an unestablished to an established position cannot be made except as a result of a competition.[3]

Promotions outside the customary course are in fact quite rare. One type of promotion which is not in the customary course, although it is of an accepted type, is from the grade of chief technical officer in a department to the grade of assistant secretary. In such cases the Civil Service Commissioners must agree to the proposed promotion, e.g., accept the promotee as qualified for appointment to the new position.

Temporary appointments, i.e., for work which is purely temporary in individual departments, are made by the minister in charge, subject to the existence of an excluding order (see p. 69) made by the Commission. Normally either a written competition or an interview is held before the names of the applicants are submitted to the minister for his approval. A temporary civil servant's services can be terminated by his department, subject to the provisions of the Minimum Notice and Terms of Employment Act 1973.[4]

The competitions held by the Civil Service Commission for the established and unestablished posts referred to above may be of various kinds and the 1956 Act gives the Commission wide scope in this matter. Section 15 (3) reads:

> Every competition shall consist of such one or more of the

---

3. *Report of Public Services Organisation Review Group 1966–1969*, par. 8.3.3.
4. Minimum Notice and Terms of Employment Act 1973 (no. 4).

following types of test as the Commissioners direct—(a) a written examination, (b) an oral examination, (c) an interview, (d) a practical examination, (e) any other test or tests considered by the Commissioners to be appropriate.

Some of these tests may be qualifying only; that is to say, there is no order of placing between candidates who reach the qualifying standard. Others may be competitive and the marks determine the order of merit. Obviously, at least one of the tests must be competitive but the Act provides that no more than one of them need be so.

Before they hold a competition, the commissioners are obliged under section 16 of the Act to make regulations governing the kinds of tests they are going to apply, what kinds of persons are eligible to compete, and so on. In preparing the regulations for posts in professional, technical or departmental grades, the Commission is advised by the department in which the officers will be employed. Since the Minister for the Public Service has statutory responsibility for all personnel matters, the regulations made by the commissioners must be approved of in advance by the minister.

Generally the recruitment activities of the Commission fall into two broad categories: (i) the recruitment of school-leavers, who are appointed mainly on the basis of written tests, though increasingly persons successful in the tests must also undergo an interview, and (ii) the recruitment of persons with professional or technical qualifications or with prescribed experience, who are selected after interviews, occasionally supplemented by practical tests. These competitions are generally referred to as open competitions, that is open to everyone who fulfils the prescribed conditions. A former Civil Service Commissioner has described in detail how the Commission operates.[5]

For each competition by interview a special and separate interview board is set up. Normally there are three persons on the board but sometimes, when more senior posts are being filled, there are as many as five. Over the years the Commission has built up an extensive panel of interviewers from all sections of the community. In inviting members of this panel to serve on an interview board, con-

---

5. Séamus Gaffney, "Recruitment to the Irish Civil Service", *Irish Banking Review*, March 1969, 19–31.

sideration is given to their special knowledge of the post, the likelihood of their being associated with the candidates to be interviewed, the probability of the person having the time to act on the board, and other relevant matters. A detailed scheme of marking is usually provided by the Commission for each board, so as to provide a framework within which it may make its assessments. When the candidates have been seen and their assessments reviewed, the board divides them into two categories: those whom they can recommend as suitable for appointment and those whom they cannot. They then submit a confidential report to the commissioners setting out the candidates in the first category in order of merit and showing the marks awarded. Persons on this list who are not successful, because there are insufficient jobs available, are not given their placings. The Commission feels that to impart such information would be incompatible with the present interview system, mainly because it feels that board members might not be so ready to make their services available if they were likely to be drawn into subsequent recriminations concerning the placing or assessment of candidates. Besides, the normal practice in the commercial world is that, after an interview, candidates are told merely whether they are being offered a job or not.

In addition to holding competitions for persons coming into the civil service for the first time, the Civil Service Commission also holds written competitions for persons already in the service who apply for posts higher than those they already hold. These are called confined competitions and are, in effect, promotions which apply mainly to the general service basic entry grades, i.e. clerical assistant, clerical officer, executive officer and administrative officer. While such promotions are the function of the Department of the Public Service, the Civil Service Commission acts as an agent for that department because of its experience and expertise in the holding of written competitions. Sometimes the competitions are by interview only and these are arranged by the department itself. The frequency of the competitions, the conditions for entry, whether the competition is to be a written one or by interview, and the number of places to be offered, are generally arranged between the staff associations and the department. Special circulars announcing the competitions are sent by the Department of the Public Service to all other departments and offices.

The governing legislation is fairly specific on the requirements which have to be fulfilled before the Commissioners can accept a person as qualified for appointment to a post for which a competiton is held. Mainly, the Commissioners must be satisfied that the person (a) has the necessary knowledge and ability, (b) is within the age limits, if any, (c) is in good health and free from physical defect or disease which could prevent him from doing the job properly and (d) is suitable on grounds of character. The requirements at (a) are tested by the examination, interview or in such other way as the regulations prescribe. As for the rest, the Commissioners do not check up on candidates at the point of application for the competition. There is no point in undertaking unnecessary work in 'clearing' a candidate in relation to the requirements at (b), (c) and (d) . . . until it becomes evident that his standard at (a) is such that he is in line for a post. A birth certificate will then be looked for as evidence of age and routine enquiries will be made to see that the candidate's character is good. It may be necessary to verify that the candidate has, in fact, the qualifications and experience which are necessary or for which he was given credit by the interview board and which affect his placing in the competition. While these enquiries are proceeding the candidate is medically examined. If everything is in order the candidate is then formally assigned or recommended for appointment to the department concerned.[6]

It may be of interest to mention the post of chief medical officer for the civil service which was created in 1923. Originally the post was designated as chief medical officer for the General Post Office and, indeed, the incumbent continues to have his office in the GPO in Dublin. In addition to his 'Post Office' duties, he was to act in an advisory capacity for other government departments on matters relating to the health of staff and the sanitary conditions of government buildings. Over the years his range of duties has broadened to embrace the whole civil service and the post is now known as chief medical officer for the civil service. The appointment is made after a competition held by the Civil Service Commission. The holder of

6. ibid., p. 29.

the post is formally designated as (i) chief medical officer for civil service staff generally and particularly for the staff of the Department of Posts and Telegraphs; (ii) medical adviser to the Civil Service and Local Appointments Commissions with responsibility for carrying out any medical examinations that may be requested by these bodies; (iii) medical adviser to the prisons service; (iv) medical adviser to the Minister for Education on matters relating to the appointment, sick leave and superannuation of teachers and trainee teachers. In addition, he is called upon to carry out such other duties as may be assigned from time to time by direction of the Minister for the Public Service.

In order to save candidates the expense of travelling to Dublin to undergo medical examination, the chief medical officer nominates doctors in rural areas to carry out medical examinations for the Civil Service and Local Appointments Commissions and for the various departments which employ temporary staff. He also advises heads of departments on matters relating to the suitability of their staff for promotion and on various other occasions where an officer's health record must be considered.

The legal position regarding the appointment of staff who have been recommended by the Civil Service Commissioners and pronounced fit by the chief medical officer, is that, under Section 20 of the Ministers and Secretaries Act 1924,[7] the minister in charge of a department is employer of all staff in that department. Accordingly, the names of persons selected by the Commission are submitted to departments to procure the minister's approval to the appointment. No alternative names are provided and departments invariably appoint the persons recommended by the Commission. In practice, the names of persons selected for appointment to the basic general service grades are not submitted to the minister.

Under Section 5 of the Civil Service Commissioners Act, the Commission has the power to make an order declaring that any specified post shall be "an excluded position" for the purpose of the Act. The effect of this is that the department may then fill the post in whatever way it thinks best, whether by written examination or by interview.

---

7. Ministers and Secretaries Act 1924 (no. 16).

An excluding order is, of course, only made at the request of the minister in charge of the department concerned and provided that the Minister for the Public Service agrees. The formal procedure is that the employing department writes to the Department of the Public Service setting out why it is necessary that a particular post should not be filled by the normal Commission procedures. In other words, it has to justify the filling of a post in this way. The reasons may be that staff are required urgently and that the statutory procedures are too slow to enable vacancies to be filled sufficiently quickly, or that the persons are required for a short period or, perhaps, it may be the desirability of appointing local staff to a local office. When the Minister for the Public Service has approved the request, the employing department must approach the Civil Service Commission to make the order. If the commissioners agree, they will make the excluding order, which will be valid for a certain period only. At the end of this period the order lapses, and the department concerned no longer has any legal authority to retain in its employment the person or persons covered by the order. However, the department may apply to the Commission to have the order renewed. The commissioners do not normally favour excluding orders and generally press departments to abide by the accepted recruitment procedures.

The tables at appendices 5 and 6 are taken from the Devlin report. These show the recruitment and selection procedures of the Civil Service Commission for the main types of competition and a typical timetable for an interview competition, at the time when the report was prepared in 1969. The position has not substantially altered since then, except that the numbers of candidates coming forward have greatly increased. Commenting on these procedures, the report notes that:

> Most of the procedures are necessitated by the requirements of statute and, through their rigid procedures, the Civil Service Commission and the Local Appointments Commission have, by keeping influence out of appointments, produced an incorrupt service. There is a universal belief in the integrity and fairness of the Commissioners and any measures to improve recruitment procedures must retain public confidence in the system.[8]

---

8.   Op. cit., par. 8.3.14.

The Ministers and Secretaries Act 1924 assigned responsibility for the Civil Service Commission to the Department of Finance; on the passing of the Ministers and Secretaries (Amendment) Act 1973, this responsibility devolved on the Department of the Public Service. Parliamentary questions in relation to the activities of the Commission are answered by the Minister for the Public Service. Such questions are asked infrequently and usually relate to matters of a general nature rather than to specific cases.

Persons who wish to get particulars about vacancies in any civil service grade, and details about age limits and qualifications, may obtain this information by writing to the Secretary of the Commission at 1 Lower Grand Canal Street, Dublin.

Promotion

Promotions are, technically at any rate, appointments just as much as first appointments and are therefore also governed by the Ministers and Secretaries Act 1924, i.e., they are made (unless some special statutory provision applies) by the minister in charge of the department concerned. Promotions to more senior posts require, in addition, the concurrence of the Minister for the Public Service. The Civil Service Commissioners Act 1956 also provides for promotions, but exempts them from the requirement that selection must be made by competitions conducted by the commissioners. However, where promotion is not in the 'customary course', i.e., not in the normal grade sequence as accepted by the commissioners, the officer can be promoted only if the commissioners have been satisfied as to his knowledge, ability and health, and if they issue a certificate to the effect that the officer is qualified for appointment to the new position. An officer cannot, however, be promoted from an unestablished to an established position unless he succeeds at a competition held by the commissioners.

The principle is laid down that officers seeking promotion should be selected on merit. Before an officer can be promoted, the head of the department must certify that the officer is not alone fully qualified for the vacant position but is also the best qualified of all the officers eligible for it. It is left to each head of department to decide the method of selecting the most meritorious officer. Some departments hold formal competitions, usually of the interview board type; others use less formal means of comparing the merits of the candidates, such as consultations with senior officers. However, there is an obligation to review the entire field and pick the officer who can be recommended as the best qualified. All promotions require the approval of the appropriate minister.

Sometimes the net is cast wider than the officers serving in the department in which the promotion vacancy exists. In that event, applications are invited from all departments and a board of senior officers, including normally at least one from a department other than that in which the vacancy exists, is set up to review the field of candidates and recommend the most suitable. In a few cases applications are invited from all qualified persons, both inside and outside the service, and a special interview board, including non-civil servants, is set up. This was the procedure adopted for appointing some of the higher officers to the newly-created Department of the Public Service.

In addition to his ability to perform the duties of the higher grade, an officer recommended for promotion must also have a satisfactory health and conduct record. In some instances, particular qualifications for promotion may be prescribed, such as minimum service in a lower grade, possession of an academic qualification, or success at an examination set by the department.

Many promotions are in the first instance classified as 'acting', i.e., the promotion is temporary and may be terminated at any time. The officer is later confirmed in his promotion only if his performance during the 'acting' period has been satisfactory.

While it would be unfair to say that promotion prospects are an obsession with civil servants, it would be reasonable to say that they are never far from their minds. Ralph Christopher writes "Promotion is a race like any other and its results are accepted in the degree to which the contest is fair."[9] Discussing the problems of selection, he points out that

It is axiomatic that attitudes to promotion systems will follow perceived interests. The senior candidate will tend to see not merely convenience but even manifest wisdom in the principle of

---

9.   Ralph Christopher, "Promotion Policy", *Administration*, XXI, 3 (1973), 345.

seniority. The junior man will be no less convinced that the merit principle is part of the very order of nature. This clash of view is natural and inevitable.[10]

The various problems of selection and promotion figure largely in the ongoing discussions between staff associations and management on all aspects of personnel policy.

---

10. ibid., p. 346.

Chapter Six

Pay and Superannuation

The great majority of civil servants are remunerated on scales of pay which contain provision for a number of annual increments. This system of payments precedes even the 1854 Northcote-Trevelyan Report on the Organisation of the Permanent Civil Service. That report noted that the advance of salaries in the public service was regulated by two principles—annual increments and promotion to a higher grade. On increments, the report stated:

> Each man, on being appointed to a clerkship in a particular class, receives for the first year, and in some cases for the first two or three years, what is called the minimum salary of that class, after which his salary increases, by a certain annual increment, to what is called the maximum salary. . . . The theory of the public service is that the annual increase of salary, from the minimum to the maximum of the class, is given as a matter of course as the reward of service, and with no reference to the comparative merits of the individuals. . . .

The report went on:

> With regard to the annual increase of salary, we are of opinion that it would be right to require that each clerk, before becoming entitled to receive the addition, should produce a certificate from his immediate superior, that he has been punctual in his attendance, and has given satisfaction in the discharge of his duties, during the preceding year. Such certificates are required from the heads of rooms in the Ordnance Department, and from each Inspector in the Audit Office. They would ordinarily be given as a matter of course, but the knowledge that they

might be withheld would be useful in maintaining discipline, and in enforcing regularity of attendance, which in some cases is a matter of difficulty, the only penalties which can at present be imposed for irregularity being those of suspension and dismissal, which are too severe to be applied unless in aggravated instances.[1]

In its factual memorandum, submitted almost exactly a hundred years later to the Priestley Commission,[2] the Treasury stated:

The Civil Service pay structure is normally characterised by
  (i) short scales for non-office grades such as messengers, cleaners and post office engineering labourers, and some of their supervisors;
  (ii) long scales for many basic or recruitment grades, e.g. the executive officer or works group basic grade;
  (iii) medium length scales for office staff in the middle ranges;
  (iv) short scales for office staff in the higher ranges—culminating in flat rates at the highest levels.
In this context 'short' means scales from two to six points (both figures included) for adult males; 'medium' means scales from six to ten points; and 'long' means scales with ten or more points.[3]

In the same memorandum the Treasury set out the procedure adopted when new scales had to be devised. It stated that the size and number of the increments proposed had been designed to achieve one or more of three main purposes: (i) to provide a suitable annual reward, (ii) to produce a scale of suitable length, (iii) to make the assimilation increases accruing at different points on the old scale as equitable as possible: "One would not therefore expect to find any standardised incremental pattern throughout the Civil Service. And in fact this is so. Thus at the same salary level, increments will vary as between different classes."

---

1. *Report on the Organisation of the Permanent Civil Service February 1854* (London: HMSO, 1854) C. 1713. Reproduced in *Public Administration*, XXXII, 1 (1954), 1–16.
2. *Royal Commission on the Civil Service 1953–55* (London: HMSO, 1955), Cmd. 9613.
3. *Royal Commission on the Civil Service 1953. Introductory Factual Memorandum on the Civil Service* (London, HMSO, 1954), par. 162.

The position with regard to incremental scales in the Irish civil service has not radically altered since then. There have, of course, been some minor changes; for example, a reduction in the incremental span for the executive officer grade has led to a similar reduction in the span for grades with which the executive grade has been traditionally linked. Further, the introduction of percentage and flat rate pay increases under the national pay agreements has led, in effect, to incremental scales being expressed largely in terms of a series of pay points.

The Fulton committee felt that, while up to a senior level the system of annual increments should continue, it was important that there should be more flexible progression through a pay scale: "Fixed annual increments, in our view, do not give enough incentive to effort, and make possible too easy a progress for those who do not pull their full weight."[4] Its report recommended that: "(a) additional increments should be granted both for especially good work and for success in gaining relevant qualifications, (b) increments should be withheld when they have not been earned."

Above a senior level (which level was not clearly identified), the committee said that a system of regular annual increments seemed to them unsuitable and the numbers were small enough to make a different system practicable:

> The range of pay for each grade should in effect become a 'band' of pay, in which only the maximum and minimum points for each grade would be published, and the progress of each officer through the band would not be on a regular incremental basis but determined by an annual review of his performance.[5]

The Devlin committee touched on the subject of increments but made no specific recommendation:

> In the civil service, special rewards or special increments are not given for exceptional performance. At the present stage of civil service thinking, it is not realistic to think that the system of incremental scales could be replaced by a system of merit

4. Op. cit., par. 229.
5. ibid., par. 229.

rating and of differing annual increases. The average efficient and diligent officer should be granted his increment but no increment should be granted where the standard of performance has not been certified to be fully satisfactory. At the moment, it appears to us that increments are too readily granted.[6]

It seems, then, that the system of incremental scales derives in the main from a presumption that a person's effectiveness in a new job is at its lowest when he enters it and that he should be rewarded year by year as his responsibilities increase and as he is able more effectively to discharge the full range of duties of the post. The system also appears to be designed to provide incentives, as well as having certain disciplinary connotations. Before an increment is granted, the head of the department must certify that the officer has performed his duties satisfactorily in the preceding twelve months: in practice, what this means is that the certification of an officer's superior must be countersigned by the head of the department or by someone on his behalf, normally the head of the personnel division.

As indicated above, basic, or entry, grades tend to have longer scales than promotion grades. For example, an executive officer scale has fifteen increments while a higher executive officer scale has eight. The entry grade for civil engineers has a scale with fourteen increments while the first promotion grade has a scale with eight. In general, the higher an officer proceeds in the civil service hierarchy, the smaller the number of increments on the scale and the greater the size of the increment. Civil service scales of pay and increments are set out in the *Directory of State Services* which also gives full details of the staffing arrangements of every department.[7]

The pay structure of the civil service is probably less flexible than the pay arrangements in ordinary commercial employment. Each scale is intended to represent an impersonal evaluation of the duties of the grade and the level of remuneration necessary to attract and retain people with the qualities and qualifications required for that grade. In general, the main external incentive to a civil servant to apply his best efforts to his work is the prospect of promotion and

---

6. Op. cit., par. 14.7.11.
7. See chapter 4, footnote 3.

the knowledge that, unless he gives of his best, he is unlikely to achieve higher ranking and thus a higher scale of pay.

A civil servant who is promoted to a higher grade normally enters the higher scale at his existing pay plus one increment on the new scale, or at the minimum of the higher scale, whichever is the greater. If he has been on the maximum of the old scale for three years or more, he gets two increments on the new scale, unless the new minimum is higher than that. Officers in some basic grades (for example, administrative officers) may be promoted well before they reach the maximum; on promotion, they receive considerable salary increases. Large increases of this order are, however, unusual.

Overtime is paid to general service grades up to and including the level of higher executive officer and also to some departmental grades up to about the same level of pay. Overtime is also paid to many technical grades. There are some other technical grades whose conditions of appointment do not provide for a specified number of hours attendance. In practice, however, such officers work for the same weekly hours as those in the general service grades and, if called upon to work for appreciably longer hours than these, are compensated by *ex gratia* payments. Gratuities are also paid occasionally for special reasons, such as temporary performance of higher duties, performance of duties outside those normal to the grade, especially meritorious services, and so on. Another special form of civil service remuneration is an allowance usually paid for the performance of special duties such as private secretary to a minister or to a secretary of a department.

Determination of Pay Levels

The civil service is divided into three broad groups for the purpose of determining pay. The first, and by far the largest group, is that comprehended within the conciliation and arbitration scheme for the civil service. (A summary of the scheme is given at appendix 7.) In the operation of the scheme, great reliance is placed on outside comparisons and internal relativities. The second largest group is that known as the industrial civil service; it comprises that body of workers in the skilled, semi-skilled and unskilled categories whose pay is traditionally related to the rates paid to workers in these categories who are employed outside the civil service. The smallest group is the higher civil service, consisting of the grades above those covered by the conciliation and arbitration scheme.

Any account of the principles which determine civil service pay or, to be more precise, the pay of two broad groups of civil servants (the clerical recruitment grades and the grades in the higher civil service) is indebted to two recent reports. One is the Quinn report.[8] This report indicated that, of the various standards commonly applied in wage and salary determination, the 'rate for the job' principle seemed to be the primary one which should correctly and justly be applied in the public sector. "From this it follows that pay must be determined primarily by work content and value and that a systematic comparison of the work of the grades concerned is essential."[9]

The other report is that of the Review Body on Higher Remuneration in the Public Sector.[10] Having stated boldly in paragraph 7 that "There is no scientific method of determining pay", the report goes on to discuss the criteria which are in practice used:

Whatever the machinery for fixing pay at any level, and however formal or informal it may be, the criteria used are many and varied. These criteria include (i) comparison with pay movements or with current rates in other employments and the related question of supply/demand, (ii) cost-of-living changes, (iii) changes in national productivity, past or projected, (iv) the performance of the employees concerned, (v) internal relativities, i.e., relationships within the employment concerned and (vi) the national interest. In the course of negotiations at national or local level some or all of these criteria and perhaps other criteria may be taken into account and the variety of combinations in which they are used can be great.[11]

These criteria are the same for Britain as for Ireland and both the Quinn and the Review Body's reports bear evidence of a close

---

8. *Report of the Tribunal of Inquiry into the Rates of Remuneration Payable to Clerical Recruitment Grades in the Public Sector of the Economy* (Dublin: Stationery Office, 1966), Pr. 8887.
9. ibid., par. 36.
10. *Review Body on Higher Remuneration in the Public Sector* (Dublin: Stationery Office, 1972), Prl. 2674.
11. ibid., par. 11.

acquaintance with perhaps the most authoritative document available on matters relating to the pay of civil servants in these islands, namely, the report of the Priestley Commission.

The Priestley report set out the principles which, in its view, should govern the fixing of the pay of civil servants. The first of these was the principle of fair comparison, the end being "the maintenance of a Civil Service recognised as efficient and staffed by members whose remuneration and conditions of service are thought fair both by themselves and by the community they serve."[12] The Commission said:

> 'Fair comparison' as the primary principle is fair to the community at large for two reasons. First, it looks after the ordinary citizen's interest as a taxpayer. If the Government which represents him pays what other responsible employers pay for comparable work, the citizen cannot reasonably complain that he is being exploited. Equally we consider that he would agree that he could not, in the long run, obtain an efficient service by paying less.
>
> Secondly, the principle safeguards the Civil Service from political pressures. We think it will be generally accepted that the community must suffer if the present tradition is impaired whereby a non-political Civil Service carries out impartially the tasks required of it by Governments of different political complexions. A corollary of this is that in the matter of recruitment and dismissal there must be no question of patronage or manipulation of appointments and that no improper influence should be exercised by tampering with the salaries of particular posts or individuals. The State as employer must therefore limit its freedom of action, in a way that a private employer need not, to secure, particularly in the higher Civil Service, immunity from political and personal pressures. This requires that recruitment procedures leading to admission to the established Civil Service should be more formal than those outside and should not be changed at short notice; that there should be a greater degree of security of tenure than is necessarily found outside; that the salaries of all posts in the Service should be public knowledge

---

12.   Op. cit., par. 95.

and should not be susceptible of arbitrary variation; from which it follows that there must be a high degree of standardisation in pay and conditions of service. Thus the State must enter into relationships with its employees which are more formal than those in the generality of other employments, and it can have no secrets, either from the Service generally or from the public, about the pay and conditions it offers to any of its staff. It is also subject to the limitation that it cannot improve conditions for the new recruit, or for selected civil servants already in the Service, without applying the changes simultaneously to all members of the grade or class concerned. At the same time it is necessary to have a reasonable measure of flexibility in adjusting pay and conditions to meet changed circumstances. To reconcile this with the need to avoid arbitrary and unreasonable variation of the relationships between State and employee means that principles are needed to govern civil service pay and that they must be principles that can be applied consistently by successive Governments of different political complexions. We think that the principle of fair comparison in the sense in which we define it is the only primary principle that will serve the purpose.[13]

A secondary principle put forward by the Priestley Commission was that of 'internal relativities':

It is inevitable that in an organisation so closely knit as the Civil Service, in which rates of pay are standardised and are public knowledge and in which collective bargaining is highly developed, internal relativities should be regarded as a matter of importance by the staff. It is only natural that a man in considering the adequacy of his own pay should compare it with that of fellow-employees whose responsibilities or qualifications seem to him to be in any way comparable with his own, and that if the pay of those employees is improved in relation to his own he should expect to be shown good reason why this should be done.[14]

13. ibid., pars. 97–98.
14. ibid., par. 114.

Later in that same paragraph, however, the Commission point out that "to recognise the existence of this attitude is not to say that it should be encouraged", and, again, "if the civil service differentials established at any time were to be regarded as sacrosanct for all time, this might well produce results which would be incompatible with fair comparison."

With a view to the application of the fundamental principle of fair comparison, the Commission recommended the setting up of a fact-finding body on which both the management and staff sides would be represented. The Pay Research Unit was set up in 1956. Arising from its activities, *The Economist* commented in 1960: "Few people in Britain are so well organised as Civil Servants to keep their pay up with the Joneses."[15] By that time, in the journal's view, the unit had established itself as "perhaps the brightest jewel in the firmament of middle class bargaining." More recently Geoffrey Fry produced evidence to show that "over the first decade and a half following the implementation of the Priestley Report, the members of the majority of the main civil service grades subject to pay research generally did well in terms of salary increases compared with one measure of outside movements of pay, the Wages Index."[16]

At present there are three main ways in which the pay of civil servants is reviewed. These are (i) the conciliation and arbitration scheme for the civil service, (ii) a joint industrial council attached to the Labour Court, and (iii) as a result of recommendations made from time to time by the Review Body on Higher Remuneration in the Public Sector, to which reference has already been made. Prior to April 1950, the salaries and conditions of service of civil servants were entirely determined by the Minister for Finance and there was no provision for an independent investigation of, and award on, claims for increases in pay. After lengthy negotiations, the first scheme of conciliation and arbitration was completed in that year.

The scheme's purpose is to provide a means, acceptable both to the state and its employees, for dealing with claims relating to the conditions of service of civil servants and to secure the fullest co-operation between the state as employer and civil servants as em-

---

15. *The Economist*, 16 July 1960, p. 261.
16. Geoffrey K. Fry, "Civil Service Salaries in the Post-Priestley Era 1956–1972", *Public Administration*, LII, 3 (1974), 319.

ployees for the better discharge of public business. The scheme embraces all civil servants except, in broad terms, (i) general service officers with salaries in excess of the maximum of the higher executive officer scale, (ii) administrative officers and first and second secretaries in the Department of Foreign Affairs, (iii) industrial civil servants, (iv) professional, scientific, technical or other departmental civil servants serving in a grade which has a scale maximum which is more than the maximum of the assistant principal scale. What this means, in practice, is that the scheme embraces all civil servants (with a few exceptions) with salary maxima lower than the maximum of the assistant principal grade.

Claims under the scheme are made by staff associations, representative of the various grades in the civil service but, before a claim may be dealt with, the staff association putting it forward must be recognised, for the purpose of the scheme, by the Minister for the Public Service. In applying for recognition, each association must furnish a statement to the effect that it is not associated in any way with a political organisation. Recognition, once given, is liable to be withdrawn should a staff association (i) associate officially in any way with a political organisation by, for example, using the machinery of the association to collect subscriptions for such organisation, or (ii) sponsor or resort to any form of public agitation as a means of furthering claims or seeking redress of grievances which appropriately should be dealt with through the scheme. In certain circumstances, however, as when claims have been concluded without agreement being reached, staff associations may publish factual information or comment concerning the claim, or may hold meetings of members of the civil service to express their viewpoint publicly.

Civil servants attending meetings under the scheme are allowed time off with pay, though any expenses incurred in so doing must be borne by themselves or by their associations.

Claims affecting individual officers are excluded from the scheme, except where an officer constitutes a class in himself or where, though he is the only officer serving in a grade, he can be identified as belonging to a homogeneous group. Of course, individual officers thus excluded have the right to make representations to the head of their department on matters affecting their official positions.

Where no agreement can be reached on a claim, the staff association may elect to have the claim brought to arbitration. The meetings referred to are meetings of departmental councils or of the general council which are described at appendix 7. The procedure in relation to arbitration is also set out there.[17]

In order to reduce the number of cases going forward to arbitration, an arrangement was introduced in 1973 whereby claims disagreed at either general council or at departmental councils may be referred to a mediator nominated by the Minister for Labour—in practice this is a conciliation officer attached to the Labour Court —who resumes the conciliation meeting in place of the normal chairman, in a continuing effort to reach agreement.

When the claim being heard is arbitrable, both sides must agree to refer the claim to the mediator; where the claim is not arbitrable, one or other side may ask for the mediator. This mediation experiment is being watched with interest by both management and staff; if it proves effective, it will no doubt be embodied completely in the scheme.

Most members of staff associations who are closely involved in the operation of the scheme seem to be satisfied with it as a means of resolving claims, and some grades excluded from the scheme are seeking to be included. It appears that, at general council and at departmental councils, the personal relations between the management and staff sides are good. For example, both sides agree informally to eliminate delays from the operation of the scheme. Where a claim is being submitted to a council, a statement setting out the arguments on which the claim is based, and including details of appropriate comparisons, is normally furnished by the staff side to enable the management side to give their considered views on the claim at the first meeting held to discuss it.

Industrial Employees

Up to 1972 there was no formal negotiating machinery for dealing with claims relating to the pay and conditions of about 8,000 government industrial employees—mainly forestry, drainage and maintenance workers. Negotiations on matters affecting these workers were

---

17.   The scheme is reproduced almost entirely in Basil Chubb (ed.), *A Source Book of Irish Government* (Dublin: Institute of Public Administration, 1964).

conducted locally by the different government departments with the various unions on an *ad hoc* basis. To achieve consistency, consultation between the managements of the government departments took place at an inter-departmental wages advisory committee. This body made recommendations—which were subject to the consent of the Department of Finance—on pay claims from these industrial employees. Matters relating to them are now dealt with at a joint industrial council under the auspices of the Labour Court. The council evolved from a committee set up in 1969 to negotiate sick pay and pension schemes for unestablished state employees. That committee was made up of representatives of the government departments and officials of the trade unions representing state industrial employees; the chairman was the chief conciliation officer of the Labour Court.

The constitution of the council, which is modelled on the constitutions of similar councils relating to the private sector and which takes heed of the terms of the civil service conciliation and arbitration scheme, provides for a membership of twenty-four/twelve from each side. It describes the purpose of the council as being "to provide for the better discharge of public business by the promotion of orderly and harmonious relations between the parties." Questions relating to pay and conditions are discussed at the council. In the event of failure to reach agreement, there is provision for the joint reference of the matter in dispute to the Labour Court for investigation. The chairman and secretary of the council are officers of the Labour Court.

The council meets monthly and operates on the same general basis as the conciliation and arbitration scheme for the civil service. Matters relating to the pay and conditions of service of a category of worker employed in one department only are normally dealt with in direct negotiation between the department and the union concerned. Matters relating to categories of worker who are employed in more than one department are dealt with at the council.

Pay of the Higher Civil Service
Above the salary limits set for inclusion in the conciliation and arbitration scheme, there are about 2,000 civil servants, in about 200 grades, who comprise what is called the higher civil service. Their pay

is usually negotiated directly with the Department of the Public Service, by associations representing those higher civil servants who are below assistant secretary level and by informal groups representing assistant secretaries, deputy secretaries and secretaries. Up to 1969 there was no body independently to review the pay of these civil servants. In May 1969 the Review Body on Higher Remuneration in the Public Sector was established by the government as a standing body to advise it from time to time on the general level of remuneration of senior civil servants and of public servants generally who are outside conciliation and arbitration schemes, such as the chief executives of state-sponsored bodies, county managers and members of the judiciary. From various reports published by the body, it is clear that it regards comparison with current rates of remuneration in a wide range of jobs of the same level of responsibility as the main criterion to be used in the determination of the remuneration of the grades within its purview.

Superannuation

Civil Service superannuation is governed by a number of statutory provisions. The Superannuation Act 1834 [18] is the initial Act and this has been amended since by many other statutes, the most recent of which is the Pensions (Abatement) Act 1965.[19] However, the embodiment of pension terms in detail in a statute has come to be recognised as a cumbersome arrangement, involving long delays in procuring legislative authority for any change. A joint management/ staff working party was accordingly established in 1971, under the scheme of conciliation and arbitration for the civil service, to consider claims for improvements in the superannuation code; one of its recommendations was that superannuation should be put on a flexible basis similar to that governing pay and other conditions of service. This recommendation was accepted and the necessary enabling legislation is being prepared at the time of writing.

The normal retiring age for the vast majority of established civil servants is sixty-five, but a minister may require the retirement of a civil servant in his department who has reached the age of sixty. An established civil servant is eligible for the award of a pension when

---

18.   4 and 5 Will., 4. c. 24.
19.   Pensions (Abatement) Act 1965 (no. 13).

he retires, provided that he has at least five years service and is at least sixty-years of age. This latter rule is varied, however, when an officer is forced to resign owing to ill-health, or when his office is abolished, or if the retirement is to facilitate improvements in the organisation. Retirement pensions are based on one-eightieth of salary for each year of pensionable service up to a maximum of half salary. Pensions are paid by the Office of the Paymaster General and are revised on 1 July each year by reference to pay levels in force on that date. A lump sum, at the rate of three-eightieths of retiring pay per year of established service, is also payable, up to a maximum of a year-and-a-half's pay. Where an established officer, with more than five-years service, retires on health grounds, his actual service is especially enhanced for the calculation of pension and lump sum. Only a gratuity is payable to a civil servant with less than five-years service who retires because of ill health. Cases of premature retirement, on abolition of office or to facilitate improvements in organisation, are very rare. In such cases, pension and lump sum are based on actual service up to retirement but there is statutory provision for the addition of notional years of service, at the discretion of the Minister for the Public Service.

An established officer in good health, who is retiring on age grounds, may allocate part of his own pension to provide a pension for a dependant. The dependant's pension is the actuarial equivalent of the amount of pension surrendered and becomes payable on the death of the officer; where the dependant is the officer's wife, she may receive a smaller pension concurrently with his. In such cases her pension is doubled on her husband's death.

Death gratuities of established officers who die while serving are payable to their legal personal representatives. The amount of such a gratuity is three-eightieths of pay at date of death for each year's pensionable service (maximum forty years) or one year's pay, whichever is the greater. There is no qualifying period.

On 1 January 1970 a non-contributory pension scheme for unestablished officers was introduced. (Prior to then, unestablished officers did not receive a pension.) An unestablished officer who has at least five-years pensionable service and who retires at sixty-five or over, or earlier because of ill health, receives a pension which is calculated at the rate of one-eightieth of pay, less twice the contributory old age pension payable to a single man at the date of retirement, for each year of service, subject to a maximum of forty-eightieths. A lump sum at the rate of one-thirtieth of pay (without any deduction in respect of old age pension) per year of pensionable service is also payable, subject to a maximum of a year-and-a-half's pay. When an unestablished officer dies in service, his widow or legal personal representative receives a death gratuity; the amount of such gratuity is one-thirtieth of pay for each year of pensionable service (maximum forty-five years) or one-year's pay, whichever is the greater.

Although the vast majority of civil servants retire at or before the normal retiring age, there is provision for extension of service beyond sixty-five in certain circumstances, provided that the officer is considered fit to carry out his duties. The circumstances are three-fold. The first arises where the officer demonstrates that his income on retirement would be below a prescribed hardship limit (which is varied from time to time), where his health is good and where his superior officer certifies that he performs his work satisfactorily.

The second circumstance relates to the need to retain a person in the public interest. This situation would arise where an officer was engaged on a specific task which it was desirable that he should conclude before his retirement or where an officer possessed such a particular skill that to immediately replace him would be difficult. The third circumstance relates to national service in the war of independence. In this case, the hardship limits mentioned above are rather more generous. No officer may be retained beyond the age of seventy-five. On re-employment or retention in the civil service, an officer's pension is suspended or abated by reference to the current equivalent of the pay on which it was based. At the discretion of the Minister for the Public Service, this stipulation may be waived where an officer is retained in the public interest. Abatement of pension does not apply where a former civil servant is employed elsewhere in the public sector.

A widows' and children's pension scheme for the civil service was introduced in 1969. If an officer contributing to this scheme dies in service, his widow receives a pension of one-half of the pension he would have got if he had served to retiring age. If the officer dies after retirement on pension, his widow continues to get one-half of his pension. The scheme also provides for an officer's children to benefit so long as they satisfy certain age requirements. Children's benefits are calculated at the rate of one-third of the widow's pension, subject to a maximum of three children. The effect of this arrangement is that a widow with three or more eligible children gets the pension her husband would have got. A deduction of $1\frac{1}{2}$ per cent. is made from salary or wages for those participating in the scheme, plus a deduction of 1 per cent. from the lump sum payable on retirement, or the gratuity payable on death, in respect of any years of reckonable service for which deductions from pay have not been made.

A marriage gratuity is payable to established female officers recruited from competitions advertised on or before 1 February 1974 with a minimum of five-years reckonable service on the date of marriage. The gratuity is calculated at the rate of one month's pay for each completed year of service, subject to a maximum of a year's pay, and is based on reckonable service and pay up to the date of resignation or the date of marriage, whichever is the earlier. To be eligible for the gratuity, the officer must resign within two years of her marriage. Where resignation occurs after marriage, reckonable pay for the purpose of calculating the gratuity is uprated by reference to general pay increases between the dates of marriage and of resignation. Officers recruited from competitions advertised after 1 February 1974 do not qualify for marriage gratuities. However, they may qualify for preserved pension benefits. Female officers reappointed in a pensionable capacity after the date of the removal of the marriage bar (31 July 1973) must refund any marriage gratuity previously paid to them.

By virtue of such refund, pensionable service, estimated previously for marriage gratuity, will reckon along with subsequent pensionable service for superannuation purposes. Refund of the gratuity is made during pensionable service, or by deduction from death gratuity or from retiring lump sum, and is uprated by reference to the pay level corresponding at the time of repayment to that on which the original gratuity was based. In the case of reinstated widows, the refund is made by deduction from death gratuity or lump sum, and uprating does not apply.

A civil servant does not pay superannuation contributions (except for those paid at the rate of $1\frac{1}{2}$ per cent. under the widow's and children's scheme already referred to). However, in pay negotiations it has been accepted that there should be a deduction of 5 per cent. for comparison purposes from rates in other employments where there is a superannuation contribution, as, for example, in the local authority sector. Therefore, a civil servant makes a notional contribution of 5 per cent. towards superannuation but there is no superannuation fund; all superannuation payments are made from voted money. In all claims for loss of an established civil servant's services (if he is seconded to a body outside the civil service) the value of the state's contribution to his superannuation is put at 15 per cent., or $16\frac{2}{3}$ per cent. in the case of a male officer who is a member of the widows' and children's scheme.

The Devlin committee commented in some detail on superannuation:

In theory, civil servants have free superannuation but, in practice, salaries are abated by comparison with those employments which make a superannuation deduction. The civil servant, however, gets nothing if he leaves the service before he becomes entitled to a pension; the outside worker with a contributory superannuation scheme at least gets his contributions back. At a time when superannuation schemes were rare, the civil servant's pension was an attraction; now it serves to prevent movement out of the service after mid-career. An early exception to the immobilising effect of civil service superannuation policy was the principle of 'approved employment' under which a civil servant leaving the service to take up other employment which was approved by the Treasury was allowed to have his pension entitlement at the date of his leaving frozen until such time as he would have retired in the normal course. This device was suited to the stable conditions when it was introduced but, today, inflation considerably reduces its value. It remains the only superannuation benefit a civil servant can carry to a post in many state-sponsored bodies but recently arrangements have been made for reciprocity of pension rights between the civil service and approved state-sponsored bodies. There are now reciprocal pensions provisions between the civil service and local authorities and the civil service and Universities. Movement to and from local authorities is rare except for a few engineers and doctors and, of the Universities, only University College Cork has so far adopted a reciprocal pension scheme. Lack of a common superannuation scheme is one of the greatest barriers to mobility across the public service; the fact that pension rights are non-transferable and lost on early retirement also prevents movement of dissatisfied staff out of the service to areas of the economy where they might serve more usefully. We have also had complaints from professional staff that, because of their comparatively late age of entry, they cannot qualify for full superannuation benefits and that the provision for added years for pension purposes does not fully meet the problem. As the age for ending education rises generally, the superannuation provisions do not provide for a correspondingly shorter working life.[20]

Since that was written, the position has changed significantly. Many more state-sponsored bodies and all the universities, except one, have entered the system of reciprocal transfer arrangements operated under the Superannuation and Pensions Act 1963. More important, however, have been the developments arising from the recommendations of the joint management/staff working party on superannuation, referred to above. Arrangements have now been introduced whereby a civil servant who resigns after at least five-years service, and who cannot transfer his pension rights to other employment, is eligible for a preserved pension and lump sum which become payable at age sixty and which are based on service at date of resignation and reckonable pay at that date, increased by reference to pensions increases in the intervening period. The existing arrangements for transferring pension rights are being broadened to include service with the defence forces, Garda Síochána and the teaching professions. The conditions for transfers, including the method of transfer of contributions, are being examined with a view to introducing greater flexibility in areas where the existing statutory arrangements have proved too restrictive.

20. Op. cit., par. 8.3.53.

Chapter Seven

Staff Development, Including Education and Training

Management in the Public Service owes it to their employers, the tax paying public, to be cost conscious. This obligation entails more than is necessary to do a job properly. It requires that staff be trained, educated and developed to do the job well and to get satisfaction in doing it.[1]

The setting up of a manpower development section in the Department of the Public Service shortly after its establishment and the appointment of a director of manpower to head it, as recommended in the Devlin report, means that full-time attention is now being given to all aspects of staff development in the civil service, including education and training.

A committee on the post-entry education of public servants, set up under the auspices of the Institute of Public Administration,[2] considered that staff development was concerned not so much with intelligence or efficiency as with personality, with the moral characteristics of the public servant—his integrity, responsibility, initiative, resilience and so on. The higher an officer moves in the public service, the greater the call on these qualities. The committee held that these qualities exist in most officers but at varying degrees of development and that 'development' means the effort to have the characteristics

---

1. Mr Richie Ryan, Minister for Finance and Minister for the Public Service, in an address at the Institute of Public Administration, 1 November 1974.
2. *Post-Entry Education of Public Servants* (Dublin: Institute of Public Administration, 1959).

habitually displayed and used at the highest level of which an officer is capable.

In a paper prepared in 1972, the training section of the Department of Finance commented:

Development is a familiar concept today and is concerned with growth. Staff development is no exception. It relates to the growth in potential—that is in knowledge, skills, capacity, attitudes and experience—of all the employees of an organisation. It is the extent to which each individual is enabled to use his talents to best effect in the service of his Department (or of the public service, for that matter).[3]

As already indicated, each department is responsible for the pursuit of a number of objectives which constitute the reason for the department's existence. These broad objectives are broken down into lesser aims, targets, schemes and specific activities of various kinds, in more and more detail. This process is reflected in the organisation of departments, with broad policy being determined at the higher levels, while officials at other levels draw up and execute plans in more limited areas.

All the staff employed in a department are working in their various ways towards the achievement of their department's objectives. The extent to which each of them can contribute to achieving these objectives, therefore, is a matter of concern not only to personnel branches and training authorities. "It is clearly of vital importance to every manager, from first line supervisor to Head of Department, that each individual should be enabled to contribute as much as his or her capacity allows. This will not happen by itself: it must be planned for."[4]

Staff development, therefore, has a two-fold benefit. First, and perhaps more important, it helps staff to benefit themselves, since the term embraces a series of measures designed to help them achieve their full potential. It could be argued that staff who join an organisation in their early years and give to it the whole of their life's work,

---

3. *Staff Development in the Civil Service – Preliminary Memorandum* (published in *Dul chun cinn*, a journal devoted to occasional papers in O & M, Training, ADP and other activities directed towards the raising of efficiency in the civil service, no. 13, April 1972, par. 5).
4. ibid., par. 7.

frequently as much as forty-five years, are entitled to something more from that organisation than mere payment for their services. That 'something' could be characterised as the provision of the facility for each officer to achieve his full potential and develop his true capacity. In the second place, staff development helps departments to achieve their objectives since it enables them to get the best value from their human resources.

The training section (now transferred to the Department of the Public Service) referred to in the paper suggests that a staff development programme should be based on education, training (both informal and formal), career planning and on a system of motivation and appraisal. The staff associations broadly agree with this proposition. Education and training, on which much has already been written, will be dealt with later in this chapter. In the meantime some comments will be offered on career planning and on a system of motivation and appraisal.

Career Planning

"Belonging to a democratic society with a career service for its public administration officials, most of us would readily assent to two principles as an acceptable basis for our public personnel policies. One is that there should be equality of opportunity: the other is that reward should be for merit rather than for some less worthy or less relevant attribute."[5] Equality of opportunity means that the chance given to each officer to develop and advance his career is equalised. It does *not* mean that a vacancy in a promotion grade should inevitably be filled by the most senior man from the grade below. Nor does it mean that a junior should be promoted because he has had an opportunity for development not made available to others. In other words, there would be scant justification for passing over a senior man on the grounds of inferior performance, if that inferior performance were caused by lack of training, or of delegation to him, or of variety of experience which some of those junior to him had been given the opportunity of obtaining. While it is true that management in the civil service does not deliberately discriminate, it can nevertheless happen that an officer may find himself assigned at an early age to work which is challenging, inter-

---

5.   ibid., par. 65.

esting and in the public eye. If he makes a success of this, he may be selected for special training or perhaps for some other assignment which gives him a chance to shine and bring himself further to notice. For example, a young officer selected specially for duty in a minister's private office might have a head start on his colleagues when all are being considered for promotion. What would be wrong in such an event is that too many of those officers in a department who are regarded as being in the first class, might owe their position to chance opportunities, and that, while they were being specially groomed, some of their less fortunate colleagues might be given no chance to prove that they possessed equal potential for development. This is the kind of occurrence which makes many civil servants and their staff associations less than enthusiastic about systems of career planning which savour of too much selectivity.

An equitable careers policy should reward merit and not just seniority. But every officer should have an equal opportunity to display his merit and an equal opportunity to develop his talents. It is, of course, the responsibility of management to ensure that such opportunity prevails. This calls for planning to ensure, as a minimum,

> . . . that, within the relatively limited time an officer has to serve in a grade before he becomes eligible for promotion, he should have been given sufficient experience, authority and responsibility to enable him to master the most difficult work of the grade and to demonstrate his potential for promotion. That cannot be done by chance or by *ad hoc* postings which do not form part of a planned pattern.[6]

Career planning demands attention to placement (that is, to the type of work to which a person is assigned on initial appointment), to mobility, and to ensuring that adequate authority and responsibility is delegated. In recent years the Civil Service Commission has been endeavouring to match new executive officers to the vacancies existing in departments, having obtained job specifications for these vacant posts from the departments. There are, however, problems in this area. Very often young people entering the civil service

---

6. ibid., par. 74.

do not know enough about the work of the various departments to be able to make a valid choice and, besides, in their eyes some departments may seem more glamorous than others. In addition, considerable planning and classifying of posts and of skills is demanded from the departments and the necessary information may not always be available.

The term mobility has a deeper meaning than the transfer of an officer from one type of work to another to enable him find out what is done in various areas of work. Such mobility would be for the sake of knowledge and not necessarily for the sake of experience. The real argument for mobility is that it should enable an officer to develop fully, that is to make a greater contribution to the work and its objectives by giving him the opportunity to apply the skills he has acquired in his present and previous work to a greater variety of situations.

> To be a fully effective part of career planning, a policy of mobility would have to be based on a matching of the past experience and probable career pattern of each individual, on the one hand, with the knowledge, skills, attitudes and responsibility levels of various posts, on the other. It would need to transcend departmental boundaries.[7]

The traditional dilemma of mobility versus specialisation, referred to by the Fulton committee in the first two chapters of its report, besets this whole question. Administration is becoming increasingly more complex and is demanding more and more specialisation. But then it is also true that people will not develop if they are left too long on the same job. The dilemma could perhaps be resolved if one were to think of mobility as the means of giving people the experience they need to make a success of the kind of career which from time to time, following periodic review, management wishes them to pursue. An effort could then be made to estimate what knowledge and skills personnel need in the future so that they could be transferred to posts providing these in the greatest measure feasible.

Delegation, in the context of staff development, means being

---

7. ibid., par. 86.

given the responsibility to work under less close supervision, of bringing matters a stage further without referring them upwards for guidance or approval, and being answerable for the results of decisions taken. It also means being given the authority to act, or to require others to take action, on one's own initiative. It includes greater freedom to decide the best way of doing a job, or deciding a case, rather than recommending a decision. Since promotion should, and generally does, involve a marked rise in the levels of authority and responsibility of the promotee, and since persons who have had limited authority and responsibility hitherto, cannot be expected to change overnight, it follows that such persons often find themselves unable immediately to meet the challenges of their new job. Alternatively, the more confined attitudes engendered by the limited responsibilities of the previous job are brought with them into the new post. Therefore the demands which the job makes on the individual should be continuously extended.

Motivation and Appraisal

The motivation of staff—in the sense of encouraging and enabling them to give of their best and of providing them with an incentive to do so—is part of the job of all supervisors. Many do not consciously think of this; but besides, there are problems in this area too. Supervisory styles differ. So do people's reactions to attempts to motivate them. There are differences of view as to the best way to motivate staff and there is also the 'system'—the incremental scales, the lack of incentive payments, the traditionally independent and remote roles of individual personnel divisions and the hitherto more rigid controls of the Department of Finance. That the system should be so may not be entirely the fault of management. Peter Self holds that "The employees of a modern civil service tend to prefer procedures of selection, grading and promotion which are clear, uniform and standardised. Conversely they tend to oppose the idea of giving to line managers greater discretion in personnel matters."[8] In addition to the factors already mentioned which can act as motivators of

8.   P. J. O. Self, "Tests of Efficiency: Public and Business Administration", *PAC Bulletin* (published by the Public Administration Committee of the Joint University Council for Social and Public Administration, no. 11, December 1971, 38).

performance, such as delegation and career planning (as well as education and training which will be mentioned later), communications, participation and counselling are also important elements. Communication is a two-way process. On the one hand, there should be a conscious and positive policy of informing staff on all matters having a direct or indirect bearing on their own duties and on the work of the department. Sometimes supervisors do not have access to all the information which should be imparted. Yet even when they have, they do not always pass it on, unless they are so directed.

A staff development programme could embody a general commitment by top management to adopt a policy of treating information as non-confidential unless there were special reasons for not notifying staff about some matter. It could also prescribe that staff are apprised of developments affecting the activities of the department, such as changes of policy deriving from decisions taken in Brussels.

An important aspect of a communications policy is to encourage and foster a climate in which the ideas, suggestions, questions, problems and complaints of staff are dealt with in a sympathetic and positive way. This would ensure that officers who put forward ideas and suggestions which are eventually adopted would receive credit for their initiative.

Staff who have participated in framing the approach to a task are likely to be more committed to its efficient performance than if they had been merely told just to do the work. A programme of staff development would entail overt encouragement by management of consultation at all levels, whenever possible, whether on decisions to be taken, on organisation changes, or on day-to-day matters; it also would entail granting staff the maximum freedom possible to tackle jobs in whatever way they thought best: for example, the approach to be taken at a meeting, the preparation of a memorandum of fact and argument, or the manner of dealing with an indolent subordinate.

Counselling, though heretofore a much neglected activity in the civil service, can play a vital role in staff development at all levels. Periodically, supervisors should set aside time to talk with staff members about their progress, their work problems and their general needs. The purpose of counselling is to help, by frank discussion in a friendly atmosphere, to remove any obstacles to the development of staff:

Staff appraisal procedures have many different purposes. All aim at developing people and/or organisations by using information about the behaviour of people at work. All assume that an organisation will be more effective as a result of a staff appraisal procedure.[9]

Most people would agree, no doubt, that any decisions made about human behaviour at work should be based on information. Yet informal judgements made about people in work often tend to be based on evidence which is, in itself, haphazard. Such judgements may possibly derive from happenings which are untypical or possibly from hearsay remarks. "In ordinary social situations such judgements may be of little importance. In the work situation they are important, for the person being judged, and for the organisation."[10] The main purpose of a system of staff appraisal is methodically to estimate an employee's current performance and his potential contribution to his organisation. It is designed to help staff in coping with their current and future needs and to assist supervisors in carrying out their responsibilities to their subordinates. The procedure usually adopted is that a supervisor writes a report on each officer at prescribed intervals; in addition, the officer is appraised in an interview by a superior who is two grades senior to him. The report and interview are on closely prescribed lines.

Education

In 1972 two reports were published which dealt with post-entry education for civil servants. The first of these was a report of a joint staff-management working party set up by the Department of Finance (specifically, that part of it which is now included in the Department of the Public Service) as part of its exploratory work in devising a

9. G. A. Randall et al., *Staff Appraisal* (London: Institute of Personnel Management, 1972), p. 9.
10. *Memorandum on Systems of Appraisal* (Dublin: Civil Service Training Centre, 1971), par. 2.1.

programme of staff development for the civil service. The terms of reference of the working party were:

> To recommend what measures, if any, the Civil Service as employer ought to take to encourage post-entry education as part of a comprehensive programme of staff development. The Working Party will pay particular attention to any distinction it considers necessary between the needs of younger officers (e.g. under 25 years of age) and those of mid-career officers.[11]

The second report was that of another working party set up at the request of the executive committee of the Institute of Public Administration. Its terms of reference were:

> To consider and report on the educational needs of the higher public service and the provision to be made for meeting those needs: in particular to consider the manner in which third and fourth level education can contribute to improving the quality of management in the public service.[12]

The two reports thus deal with rather similar subjects from different standpoints. The second report treats of the public service as a whole and not just the civil service. For the purpose of its report, the first working party (which indicated that it was dealing with formal educational qualifications for all civil servants, and not solely for those in general service grades) divided the service into three educational categories: those who had not completed formal second-level education, those who had completed second-level education but had not proceeded further and those who had received a primary or higher degree at third-level.

In the course of its general observations, the working party said

> The Civil Service has a poor public image, particularly in the eyes of younger people. . . . To the kind of person we would wish to attract, even at a fairly low level, industry and the semi-state

---

11. "Post-Entry Education for Civil Servants", *Administration*, XX, 3 (1972), 27.
12. "The Educational Needs of the Higher Public Service", *Administration*, XX, 3 (1972), 41.

bodies offer more enticing facilities. The more able youth will take his chance at the university rather than make a once-for-all decision to enter the Civil Service. Yet the Civil Service must attract able people or the country will suffer.

To offset the disadvantages, we suggest that the Civil Service should offer inducements in other directions. Educational opportunity could be one such and in this area we recommend that the Service should be a front-runner. We would wish to cultivate an image of a Service which offers the advantages of extensive educational opportunities to new entrants . . . the recruitment emphasis should be on opportunity rather than permanency.[13]

The working party felt that a single agency should be responsible for organising an educational programme for the civil service and recommended that this agency should be the Institute of Public Administration. The programme would be controlled by a steering committee comprising representatives from the Departments of the Public Service and of Education and the staff associations. The programme should give priority to the lower grades—technical and departmental as well as general service.

The working party went on to consider the needs of the various categories of civil servants. It recommended that those officers who had been prevented from completing their second-level education before entering the service should be given an opportunity to finish it. This recommendation would apply equally to those in the technical, departmental and general service grades, so that courses could be followed in technical as well as in general education. To this end it was recommended that an organised system of educational courses be established for such officers which would include provision for part-time release during working hours. In the case of those who had completed second-level education, the working party drew attention to the expected expansion of the technological colleges into polytechnics. Thus, the working party thought that in addition to the restricted number of evening courses at the universities, a greater diversity of awards at diploma and degree level would also be made available. As a first step it recommended that a refund of fees be

13. ibid., pars. 3. 1–3.

made to those civil servants who at the time were following courses leading to a university degree and also to those following third-level diploma courses at any other institution.

The working party also referred to those cases in which facilities were already available for persons in certain areas of the civil service to take university courses:

Already, at this level, some officers are given time off with or without pay, to take certain university courses either at their own expense or with tuition fees paid. These include student engineers in the Post Office, Meteorological Assistants and Cadets doing BSc to become meteorologists. Certain sub-departments require attendance at full-time day courses related to their own activities—the Estate Duty Office is a case in point. The university scholarship scheme for young executive officers is designed to provide recruits to grades such as economist or statistician. These are worthwhile schemes and we recommend that they be extended. There are people in technical grades with the ability and the interest to acquire a professional qualification in their own work-area and they should be assisted to the limit of the educational facilities available. It is important to recognise that service experience can be extremely valuable in cases where persons from those grades are promoted to a professional status.[14]

The working party wrote as follows about those who already had primary or higher degrees:

This category divides in two, i.e. officers in the general administrative side and officers of specialist rank, e.g. engineers, architects. In regard to the specialist, there is a demand on him, in this age of vast technological change, to keep up to date on his specialism. He cannot carry the pressures of his daily work and keep up to date at the same time. Simply lightening the load of work will not do: he must have opportunity for research or for practical experience of advanced techniques. We recommend that these officers be granted, at intervals to be decided, one

---

14.   ibid., par. 5.4.

year's sabbatical leave either to take a higher degree or to get experience of advanced techniques in outside industrial undertakings. They should suffer no loss of income or of pension rights for such leave.

Officers in the general service do not require sabbatical leave. Their needs can be met by intensive courses in administration and management, but since these are training rather than educational courses—we refrain from making any recommendation.[15]

The second working party referred to above devoted the opening section of its report to what it termed "The Public Service in Transition". In this section it dwelt upon the wide responsibilities of modern government and on the changing nature of the demands made upon the public service; this analysis relied heavily upon the Devlin and Fulton reports, quoting this excerpt from the latter report:

To meet these new tasks of government the modern civil service must be able to handle the social, economic, scientific and technical problems of our time, in an international setting. Because the solutions to complex problems need long preparation, the service must be far-sighted; from its accumulated knowledge and experience, it must show initiative in working out what are the needs of the future and how they might be met. A special responsibility now rests upon the Civil Service because one Parliament or even one government often cannot see the process through.[16]

This opening section ended with the following paragraph:

These remarks in the Fulton Report have, we believe, an equal relevance to the Irish public service. They indicate the great diversity of tasks which are allotted to a modern public service. It follows that the education and development of public servants must mirror that diversity and that an extensive range of academic resources must be drawn on to that purpose.[17]

15. ibid., pars. 6. 1–2.
16. ibid., par. 1.4.
17. ibid., par. 1.5.

In the course of its own observations on the general situation, the working party indicated that it was very far from its purpose "to decry or even question the value of these pragmatic qualities which comprise the art of administration and which to their credit our public servants have down the years cultivated with a high consistency of purpose."[18] Its inquiry was also related to educational developments which would enhance and supplement those qualities. The core of the problem, as the working party saw it, was contained in the following quotation from Basil Chubb:

> The advance of the social sciences and of accounting and statistical techniques to the point where they are essential tools for policy making and management have made it vital for public services everywhere to be peopled by a more professional race than has usually been found in the higher administrative ranks of British-style civil services. Increasing numbers of senior officers have to be capable of absorbing, appreciating, and using large amounts of systematic economic and social data in order to elucidate problems and to formulate adequate plans to place before their ministers. If, as in Ireland, the vast majority of senior officials are recruited at secondary school level, formidable education and training problems are posed, embracing the appropriate social sciences including management, not to be solved by programmes measured — as most have been in the past — in days or weeks, but demanding months or years.[19]

The working party went on to say:

> Education is a long-term investment and is best provided early in a person's career. The young person starting a career in the public service should have a developed sense of intellectual values which the right kind of third-level education will impart. He should have some appreciation of the contribution which the social sciences are making to human progress through inquiry into the nature of contemporary society. He should rapidly

18. ibid., par. 3.2.
19. Basil Chubb, *The Government and Politics of Ireland* (London: Oxford University Press, 1970), p. 244.

discover a community of interest and purpose with colleagues similarly placed in the public service. Above all he should draw inspiration from high standards of achievement within his own career vista so that he will raise his sights and gain in confidence and commitment. That is the very nature of a professional education. Our system of secondary education provides a basis but no more for this form of intellectual and personal development. Of course, we do not for a moment suggest that older people should be denied access to higher education. We accept the proposition that human sciences such as management and its related disciplines fall within the intellectual range of men and women who, no matter what their age, have maintained an active interest in the organisations in which they work and in the world about them.[20]

In considering the problem before it—recommending on the educational needs of the higher public service—the working party debated whether to set a course of policy somewhere between two alternatives which were readily available. The first was whether to take an incremental approach and maintain the existing mixed strategy of piecemeal measures or "to seek a fresh initiative having as a single-minded aim the rapid and comprehensive development of public administration as a profession."[21] In their judgement, the course of best advantage lay between the two alternatives but much nearer the second.

Accordingly the committee recognised that a major initiative was needed and recommended the establishment of degree courses in public administration within the existing system of higher education, to be provided by university departments of public administration. At the time of writing both universities in Dublin are considering the launching of such degree courses.

The committee, conscious of the fact that the foregoing arrangements could only apply mainly to those public servants working at university centres, adverted to the need for special efforts to provide parity of opportunity in professional education for provincial public

---

20. ibid., par. 3.6.
21. ibid., par. 3.7.

servants and recommended that the Institute of Public Administration's Diploma in Administrative Science should be developed into a degree course. This would be offered by the regional technical colleges and the National Institute of Higher Education in Limerick as well as by a correspondence course run by the Institute of Public Administration.

In addition to the primary degree in public administration, the working party suggested a master's degree in the same subject and the provision of scholarships for postgraduate studies in public administration at foreign institutions.

It also suggested that those public servants who wished to take part-time courses, such as those leading to the degrees of Bachelor of Arts or of Commerce or to becoming a barrister-at-law, should also be granted reasonable facilities by their employers.

The working party concluded by stressing a point which it regarded as vital to many of its recommendations:

> Facilities for higher education should be offered as elements in a positive programme of career development. It is not enough that facilities be granted on request; public servants must be made aware of the various opportunities for higher studies on offer and they should be actively encouraged to avail of them.[22]

It also commented on the School of Public Administration, which provides a one-year course, on a full-time basis, in government, economics and social administration, for officers in the public service and others at home and overseas wishing to enter. Suitable applicants from the public service are required to have a high standard of general education, at least two-years service in a recruitment grade, and to be of a capacity and age to derive particular benefit from advanced study. Experience has shown that the course is best suited to executive officers or their equivalents with between three- and seven-years' service.

The working party foresaw an alteration in the role of the school because of the evolution of degree courses within the main educational system. It envisaged the school developing practical orientation courses within undergraduate and postgraduate courses and,

---

22.   ibid., par. 4.12.

perhaps, preparing case studies of a high quality, thus providing teaching materials of a practical kind. It also saw this sort of 'clinical' experience as a desirable supplement to advanced academic studies, which would help to form professional attitudes among participants.[23]

Both reports were submitted to the Minister for the Public Service who announced soon afterwards that refunds of course and examination fees would be made to civil servants who, in their own time, pursue courses of study provided by a university or other educational or professional body which lead to a third-level qualification accepted as being relevant to the officers' employment in the civil service. The minister also declared that refunds on the same basis and conditions would be made in respect of second-level education and that tuition and examination fees would be refunded to officers attending approved classes at vocational schools in their own time. The remainder of the recommendations are still being examined in consultation with the staff associations. The Department of the Public Service has indicated that it is fully conscious of the need to do what it can to further the educational aspirations of civil servants. It appreciates the role which formal education plays in producing better motivated officers and, ultimately, a more efficient administration. However, it has also indicated that it realises that any facilities granted in the field of education and training must be consistent with the primary function of the civil service, namely, to provide an efficient administration.

Training

Perhaps the most comprehensive report on the training of civil servants is that prepared by the Assheton committee in Britain. One of the questions the committee asked themselves was "What is the object of training?" Having considered the question of the technical efficiency of the individual staff member and the less tangible efficiency of the organisation as a whole, deriving from the collective spirit and outlook of the individuals which comprise it, the committee suggested the following five main aims:

First, training should endeavour to produce a civil servant

---

23. ibid., par. 4.15.

whose precision and clarity in the transaction of business can be taken for granted.

In the second place, the civil servant must be attuned to the tasks which he will be called upon to perform in a changing world. The Civil Service must continuously and boldly adjust its outlook and its methods to the new needs of new times.

Thirdly, there is a need to develop resistance to the danger of the civil servant becoming mechanised by the machine; whilst we must aim at the highest possible standard of efficiency, our purpose is not to produce a robot-like, mechanically-perfect Civil Service. The recruit from the first should be made aware of the relation of his work to the service rendered by his Department to the community. The capacity to see what he is doing in a wider setting will make the work not only more valuable to his Department but more stimulating to himself. In addition, therefore, to purely vocational training directed to the proper performance of his day-to-day work, he should receive instruction on a broader basis as well as encouragement to persevere with his own educational development.

Fourthly, even as regards vocational training, it is not sufficient to train solely for the job which lies immediately at hand. Training must be directed not only to enabling an individual to perform his current work more efficiently, but also to fitting him for other duties, and, where appropriate, developing his capacity for higher work and greater responsibilities.

Fifthly, even these ends are not in themselves enough. Large numbers of people have inevitably to spend most of their working lives upon tasks of a routine character, and with this human problem ever in the background, training plans, to be successful, must pay substantial regard to staff morale.[24]

In one of his many publications on aspects of the civil service in Ireland, Basil Chubb made particular reference to the executive grades: "The problem of the preparation and training of these officers who are destined to fill key posts is one of increasing im-

---

24. *Report of the Committee on the Training of Civil Servants* (London: HMSO, 1944), Cmd. 6525, par. 16.

portance now that the role of the Civil Service in promoting and guiding the development of the community is so much greater than it was."[25]

More recently, the Fulton committee in Britain devoted several paragraphs to the subject of training:

We have said that in the more professional Civil Service of the future it will not be enough for civil servants to be skilled in the techniques of administration; they must also have a thorough knowledge of the subject-matter of their field of administration and keep up to date in it. Thus training should be designed to equip administrators. . . . Similarly, specialists need to be equipped to an appropriate degree for administration and management in addition to their normal skills in their specialism.[26]

To this end the committee recommended the establishment of a civil service college which would provide, *inter alia,* major training courses in administration and management to include (i) courses for specialists, such as scientists, engineers, architects, who need training in administration and management both early in their careers and later; (ii) post-entry training for graduates directly recruited for administrative work in the economic, financial or social areas of government; (iii) additional courses in management for officers in their thirties and forties who will become the more senior staff; (iv) refresher courses in the latest management techniques; (v) courses for the best of the younger entry to help them compete with the graduates. In addition, Fulton recommended that the college should provide a wide range of shorter training courses for a much larger body of staff. This college has been established and operates from three centres: London, Sunningdale Park and Edinburgh.

The Devlin group, who were mainly concerned with the organisation of the public service, also referred to training:

While Departments will be mainly responsible for the development of staff at the lower levels, we believe that the lack of

---

25. Basil Chubb (ed.), *A Source Book of Irish Government* (Dublin: Institute of Public Administration, 1964), p. 119.
26. Op. cit., par. 98.

management training at the higher levels is such a fundamental defect in our system that its remedy must be the responsibility of the central personnel function. Everyone who attains the rank of Assistant Secretary should have had the benefit of one or more full-time and extended courses to develop his potential and we would recommend that at any stage of an officer's career when it appears from the structure of his Department or from his exceptional talents, that he is likely to attain this rank, the fact should be made known to the Director of Manpower Development who will make arrangements in conjunction with his Department to afford him this training. Generally, training should be related to the career for which the officer seems to have a special aptitude. Furthermore, training can be divided into specialised training for Departments and the generalised training needed by all public servants. The Director of Manpower Development will be responsible for securing that Departments are devoting sufficient resources to both types of training.[27]

Post-entry training is usually regarded as consisting of formal and informal training:

By formal training is meant a process of organising training in a way which marks it off clearly from the ordinary duties of an officer: the training usually entails gathering a number of trainees together in the one place for lectures, discussions, practical exercises and that sort of thing. Informal training is a term which is given to the process of learning on the job, with the guidance and help of colleagues and superiors.[28]

Training is of two kinds, active and passive:

Passive training is the conditioning process given by experience so that responses to recurrent stimuli become predictable and almost instinctive. This aims to expose each officer to such

27. Op. cit., par. 14.3.5.
28. Séamus Gaffney, "Irish Civil Servants in Training", *Administration*, XIII, 1 (1965), 40.

variety of stimuli as will ensure that complex administrative problems will be met with adequate responses and that no part of his intellectual equipment suffers from lack of use.

Active training means imparting knowledge to the trainee through (a) a process of formal teaching, (b) his participation in guided discussions, and (c) experience gained while working under the guidance of immediate superiors.[29]

The Extent of Training

Séamus Gaffney writes that "In the general service sector, it can be said that the late 1940s saw a great heightening of the awareness that better arrangements needed to be made for training."[30] It is likely that one of the reasons for this may have been the publication of the Assheton report. Another, more proximate, reason was that in 1949 the establishment (personnel) officers of the various Irish government departments and offices began to meet periodically to discuss staff and other matters of mutual interest. One of the recommendations which emanated from these meetings was that a series of courses on management should be arranged for higher executive officers and carried out by the Department of Finance. This was, as far as can be ascertained, the first step in staff training in the Irish civil service:

Training on a service-wide basis in Ireland began with a one-week course launched in 1952 for higher executive officers. This course which is taken on promotion includes the elements of management, organisation and methods, administrative processes and staff assessment and reporting. Next came short courses for administrative officers including courses and a lecture series on economics, mathematics, input/output analysis and econometric model building; these were replaced in 1966 by a seven-week course designed to combine background knowledge of the aims, procedures and institutions of public administration with training in personal skills and some appreciation of professional disciplines. Induction training for executive

---

29. *Post-Entry Education of Public Servants*, p. 5.
30. Op. cit., 41.

officers was introduced in 1961. Courses dealing specifically with personal skills and management techniques were developed concurrently.[31]

Apart from the specialised training units in the Department of Posts and Telegraphs and in the Office of the Revenue Commissioners, which catered for the specialist technical needs of certain departmental grades, no other training was provided for civil servants up to this time.

"The first Departmental Training Officer to cater for general service grades was appointed in the Department of Agriculture in 1962."[32] This was the present writer. All departments now have the services of at least one full-time departmental training officer. A number of departments and offices have a training officer exclusively for their own training, while others, mainly the smaller ones, share such an officer. Some departmental training officers have formed groups of two or three to share duties and provide joint training programmes.

Training is provided within departments for grades from clerical assistant to higher executive officer and for analogous departmental grades. The courses deal with such topics as the background to the work and policies of particular departments or offices; effective writing; supervisory techniques; office organisation; public relations and various other matters of direct relevance to the particular grades. On-the-job training is also carried out, but to a limited extent. Of the 9,500 civil servants who attended training courses and seminars (excluding language courses) during 1971–72, more than 7,000 attended courses provided by departmental training officers.[33]

The civil service training centre is located in the Department of the Public Service. Its basic aims are "the institution and management of a service-wide staff development programme and the management and (where necessary) provision of training."[34] The training centre provides departments with information on the range of courses in

31. T. P. O'Connor, *The Higher Civil Service in Ireland: its role, recruitment and training* (Dublin University, unpublished M Litt thesis, 1967).
32. S. de Freine, *Review of In-Service Training* (Dublin: Civil Service Training Centre, 1974), par. 1.2.
33. *Civil Service Training Centre Annual Report 1971–72*, p. 2.2.
34. ibid., p. 1.1.

management and other fields of interest which are available in Ireland and elsewhere. It also provides courses for officers from higher executive officer and equivalent levels upwards.

The Institute of Public Administration runs a comprehensive training programme designed to meet the training needs of the public service as a whole, including civil servants, at significant stages in their careers. The stated objectives of its courses are:

to help to provide for the planned and progressive development and training of staffs of public bodies.

to introduce those engaged in public administration in this country to the most advanced methods and techniques of administration and management.

to help to secure the introduction and practical application of those techniques and skills which have proved most successful in increasing efficiency in other countries with which we are increasingly coming into contact.[35]

Many people question the value of training, pointing out that its results are difficult, if not impossible, to evaluate or quantify and that it must be largely regarded as an act of faith. Conscious of this scepticism, the Department of the Public Service has funded a research project to evaluate the system of formal training for the public service which is being provided by the Institute of Public Administration and by the civil service training centre. This is a three-year project due for completion towards the middle of 1977.

---

35. Institute of Public Administration, *Programme of Courses 1975–76*, p. 4.

Chapter Eight

The Regulations:
the Department of the Public Service

Because of their official positions and their close association with the processes of government, civil servants are subject to certain restrictions which do not apply to other citizens. These relate to such matters as participation in party politics and the making of public statements.

Participation in Party Politics

The regulations restricting civil servants from participating in party politics have been the subject of discussion between staff associations and the Department of the Public Service in recent years. The associations feel that their members should have the right to take a more active part in politics than is permitted to them under these regulations. Essentially, their argument is that civil servants, because of their experience of the administrative machine, are particularly well-qualified for service in parliament and that it is inconsistent with the natural rights of a civil servant as a citizen, and harmful to the public interest, if he is not allowed to offer himself for this other form of public service and to serve the community in another capacity, without being expected to sacrifice his career, security of employment and pension rights. The Department of the Public Service, on the other hand, has been apprehensive of the results of having civil servants playing an active role in party politics. Basically the problem is one of endeavouring to reconcile two conflicting principles. In framing its recommendations relating to civil servants in Britain, the Masterman committee constantly endeavoured to find a balance between these two principles. On the one hand, "in a democratic society it is desirable for all citizens to have a voice in the affairs of State and for as many as possible to play an active part in public life." On the other, "the public interest demands the maintenance of political impartiality in the Civil Service and of confidence in that impartiality as an essential part of the structure of Government in this country."[1]

The first principle is rarely argued about. It is accepted that the civil service contains as high a proportion of able persons as any sector of Irish society and that the state would benefit from their playing an active part in politics. At the same time, the public interest requires that civil servants concerned with the framing of policy proposals should serve, and be seen to serve, successive governments objectively and impartially. Equally, it is argued that it is undesirable that civil servants, whose work concerns the execution of policy and entails direct contact with the public as, for example, in the allocation of grants or of social benefits, or in the assessment of tax, should be known adherents of a particular political party or be known to have political ambitions:

> . . . the essential factor is the relation of civil servants with the public rather than their relations with the Minister. First the work of these civil servants must in fact be completely impartial. Secondly, the public as a whole and the Press must be satisfied in their own minds that no suggestion of political bias enters into their treatment of individuals. Public opinion is a sensititive barometer reacting sharply to any breaches of the traditional impartiality of the Civil Service.[2]

The problem is one of determining the extent to which considerations about the public interest should override the right to take part in political activities. The identification of civil servants with politics gives rise to a number of contingencies, such as the emergence of a political pressure group on behalf of civil service interests and a demand from supporters of the government of the day for the spoils system of appointments. The Masterman committee had this to say about the latter aspect:

> There is finally to be considered the harmful effect upon the Service itself if the political allegiance of individual civil servants

---

1. *Report of the Committee on the Political Activities of Civil Servants* (London: HMSO, 1949), Cmd. 7718, par. 37.
2. ibid., par. 42.

became generally known to their superior officers and colleagues. If a Minister began to consider whether A, on account of his party views, might be more capable of carrying out his policy than B, the usefulness of B would be limited and the opportunities of A would be unfairly improved. This would become known, and a tendency to trim the sails to the prevailing wind would be one consequence. Another would be a cynicism about the reasons for promotion, very damaging to morale.[3]

The practice in Britain and Ireland differs from that in a number of other European countries. In Sweden, for example, even senior civil servants are allowed to pursue political activities and many members of the Riksdag, both from the government and the opposition, are civil servants. They maintain their posts in the service and are granted leave when parliament or its committees are sitting.[4] Indeed, the Swedish Constitution provides that at least two ministers must have held civil office. This requirement was originally designed to ensure that the Council of State had the services of ministers with a high degree of legal and administrative expertise.

In France also, civil servants have the right to stand for election, although they cannot sit in parliament while remaining active in the service, nor can they be promoted during their term of office in parliament. "The Government even attempts to encourage candidates, and an official circular, which rests on no legal foundation, has granted civil servants who are parliamentary candidates leave on full pay for the period of the electoral campaign."[5] If they so desire they must be taken back into the civil service when they lose their seats.

Early in 1974 the Irish government decided to modify the existing restrictions on political activity in the case of 80 per cent. of civil servants. The effect of this decision is that two main categories of staff are now free to engage in politics but not to stand for parliament. These include about 15,000 employees of the Department of Posts and Telegraphs, such as clerks, telephonists, postmen, sorters,

---

3.   ibid., par. 43.
4.   Neil C. M. Elder, *Government in Sweden* (Oxford: Pergamon Press, 1970), p. 42.
5.   Roger Gregoire, *The French Civil Service* (Brussels: International Institute of Administrative Sciences, 1964), p. 361.

technicians and labourers as well as some 8,000 industrial staff such as forestry and drainage workers. They also include about 10,000 clerical workers and analogous grades in the technical area who are free to take part in politics, subject to a proviso that the Minister for the Public Service, on the recommendation of the minister in charge of a particular department, might declare that such freedom should not apply to officers engaged on a particular category of work. The proviso relates to groups and not to individuals. Civil servants involved in the framing of policy proposals remain completely barred from political activity. This embargo embraces the executive, middle and senior grades.

The text of the statement issued by the Government Information Services on the occasion of the announcement of the government's decision is at appendix 8.

Outside Occupations

Although civil servants, other than those in professional grades, are not prohibited from taking on other work (including work for remuneration) outside official hours, they must exercise reasonable precautions (including any necessary consultation with the head of their department, where there is doubt) that their outside activities do not conflict with their official duties and are not of such a nature as to hinder the effective performance of such duties. For example, an officer would probably be precluded from doing outside work for a firm which did business with his department or from taking up an occupation which involved work during the night. If there is any danger of a conflict of interests, the officer is expected to reveal the full facts to the head of his department and abide by the latter's decision in the matter. The conditions of service of professional officers, such as architects and engineers, usually specifically prohibits them from engaging in private practice or from having connections with outside businesses.

Strike Action

Section 9 of the Offences against the State Act 1939[6] states that a person who incites or encourages any person employed in any

---

6. Offences Against the State Act 1939 (no. 4).

capacity by the state to refuse, neglect or omit (in a manner or to an extent calculated to dislocate the public service or a branch thereof) to perform his duty or who aids, abets or conspires with another person towards this end, is guilty of an offence punishable by imprisonment. The extent to which this provision might be successfully relied upon by management in the case of industrial action by civil servants would, no doubt, depend on the nature and circumstances of the action.

Under Section 16 of the Civil Service Regulation Act 1956, payment is prohibited for periods of unauthorised absence. Absence during a strike would, of course, be unauthorised absence. Attendance at the place of work, but complete refusal to do any work appears to be, in effect, unauthorised absence.

Official Secrets

The obligations of civil servants in relation to secrecy in the transaction of official business are embodied in Section 4 of the Official Secrets Act 1963.[7] Under the Act, a civil servant is prohibited from communicating official information, unless he is authorised to do so in the course of, and in accordance with, his official duties, or where it is his duty to communicate it in the interests of the state. Official information is defined in the Act but, broadly, it embraces all information which a civil servant learns in the course of his duty. It includes not only documentary material such as departmental papers, minutes, memoranda, briefs, letters and so on, but also views, opinions, comments and advice acquired or transmitted verbally. Civil servants may not make unauthorised communications either directly or indirectly on matters which come to their notice in the course of their official duties, and are obliged to refrain from mentioning such matters to anyone other than in the course of such duties.

In practice, the disclosure of official information by civil servants is governed by a doctrine of implicit authorisation: where a minister does not explicitly direct that certain official information should not be disclosed to persons outside, authorisation for disclosure by a civil servant is held to be implicit. Senior civil servants, in particular,

---

7.   Official Secrets Act 1963 (no. 1).

exercise a considerable degree of personal judgement in deciding what official information they may disclose and to whom: ". . . it is acknowledged that there is a 'line' over which a civil servant should not step, a line which protects the integrity of the cause he is serving in the Civil Service. While the 'line' is difficult to define, senior civil servants rarely experience difficulty in practice in knowing when they are approaching it."[8] The prohibition referred to also applies to persons who have retired from public office: they cannot divulge official information which they obtained or to which they had access before retirement.

Further, a civil servant may not publish, without the agreement of the head of his department, any material touching on the business of his own or other departments. If permission is granted, it is on condition that the writer must accept the terms on which copies of the work are supplied to the Stationery Office, if it is likely to be required for use in the civil service.

Integrity

Also governing the activities of civil servants are the provisions of the Prevention of Corruption Acts 1889–1916, as adapted by the Adaptation Order No. 37 of 1928. Any person holding an office remunerated out of the central fund, or out of moneys provided by the Oireachtas, is guilty of a misdemeanour punishable by imprisonment or fine, or both, if he (i) corruptly accepts or obtains, or agrees to accept or attempts to obtain, from any person, any gift or consideration as an inducement or reward for doing or forbearing to do, or for having done or forborne to do, any act in relation to the affairs or business of his department, or for showing or forbearing to show favour or disfavour in relation to such affairs or business; or (ii) corruptly gives or agrees to give or offers any gift or consideration as an inducement or reward for doing or forbearing to do, or for having done or forborne to do, any act in relation to the affairs or business of the state, or for showing or forbearing to show favour or disfavour to any person in relation to the affairs or business of the state; (iii) knowingly uses, with intent to deceive the head of his

---

8.   Maurice Wright, "The Reponsibility of the Civil Servant in Great Britain", *Administration*, XXIII, 4(1975), 365.

department, any receipt, account or other document in respect of which his department is interested, and which contains any statement which is false or erroneous or defective in any material particular, and which to his knowledge is intended to mislead.[9]

Where it is proved that any money, gift, or other consideration has been received by a person holding an office remunerated out of the central fund or out of moneys provided by the Oireachtas, from a person or agent of a person holding or seeking to obtain a contract from a government department, the same is deemed to have been received corruptly as such inducement or reward as mentioned in the Acts, unless the contrary is proved.

Anonymity

Under the Ministers and Secretaries Act 1924, each minister, as head of his department, is a corporation sole with perpetual succession and an official seal. The effect of these statutory provisions is that the acts of a department are the acts of its minister. "Unless there is a statutory exception no civil servant can, in law, give a decision."[10] Accordingly, "When, in law, the Minister is the Department, his servants have no separate existence and every statement by the Department issues from the Minister or on his behalf."[11] As a result, in this system the civil servant is anonymous and is seen as only a background figure. This has been the traditionally accepted situation. The civil servant receives neither credit nor blame for any of his actions. However, this situation is changing, partly because of the pressures of the press, radio and television. The reason for the change lies partly in the demand for wider and more open consultation with interested parties before decisions affecting the public are taken by government departments, resulting in individual civil servants becoming known personally to a wider range of people with whom their departments have official dealings. It lies partly in the breaking down of the convention that only a minister should explain issues in public and what actions his department is taking in relation to them:

---

9. Prevention of Corruption Act 1906, Chapter 34. Section 1 (1).

10. *Report of Public Services Organisation Review Group 1966–69*, par. 4.1.9.

11. ibid., par. 10.7.1.

This convention has depended in the past on the assumption that the doctrine of ministerial responsibility means that a Minister has full detailed knowledge and control of all the activities of his department. This assumption is no longer tenable. The Minister and his junior Ministers cannot know all that is going on in his department, nor can they nowadays be present at every forum where legitimate questions are raised about its activities. The consequence is that some of these questions go unanswered.[12]

Maurice Wright argues that British ministers no longer accept responsibility for all the actions of their civil servants:

Ministerial responsibility has come to mean that they are expected to accept responsibility for those policies, and issues of policy, which they personally, or their civil servants on their instructions, have initiated, developed or carried through. They are no longer expected to accept responsibility for those culpable actions of their civil servants of which they had no prior knowledge and of which they disapprove. Nor are they expected to accept responsibility for those errors or delays of their civil servants which do not involve an important issue of policy. Thus, what Ministers can properly be held responsible for has been considerably circumscribed in recent years; conversely, civil servants are now liable to be held responsible for a wider range of issues.[13]

In support of his argument, Wright refers to the recent case in Britain where a failure of departmental management resulted in delay in dealing with an important piece of business which had passed through the hands of ministers and several senior civil servants. The head of the division within the department was held responsible by a tribunal of inquiry and found guilty of incompetence and negligence. His immediate superiors, including the permanent

12.   *The Civil Service, Vol. I. Report of the Committee 1966–68* (London: HMSO, 1968), Cmnd. 3638, par. 283.
13.   Op. cit., 374.

secretary, together with the ministers of successive governments who had been involved, were absolved from all blame.[14]

Anonymity is, of course, a requirement in the Irish civil service. Chubb writes: "In respect of public affairs, civil servants have to seek permission to publish or appear on radio or television and, in practice, have often found it quite hard to get it, even for innocuous material."[15] The Devlin report made no recommendations on this matter, except to state the convention. However, the Fulton report did comment:

> In our view, therefore, the convention of anonymity should be modified and civil servants, as professional administrators, should be able to go further than now in explaining what their departments are doing, at any rate so far as concerns managing existing policies and implementing legislation.
>
> We do not underestimate the risks involved in such a change. It is often difficult to explain without also appearing to argue; however impartially one presents the facts, there will always be those who think that the presentation is biased. It would be unrealistic to suppose that a civil servant will not sometimes drop a brick and embarrass his Minister. We believe that this will have to be faced and that Ministers and MPs should take a tolerant view of the civil servant who inadvertently steps out of line. On balance we think it best not to offer any specific precepts for the progressive relaxation of the convention of anonymity. It should be left to develop gradually and pragmatically. . . .[16]

A permanent undersecretary of state in the Ministry of Defence in Britain said that, while he had a good deal of sympathy with the view of the Fulton committee, his own experience made him dubious about the extent to which permanent secretaries could in practice

---

14. *Report of the tribunal appointed to inquire into certain issues in relation to the circumstances leading up to the cessation of trading by the Vehicle and General Insurance Company Limited* (James Tribunal) H.L. 80, H.C. 133 (London: HMSO, 1972).
15. Basil Chubb, *The Government and Politics of Ireland* (London: Oxford University Press, 1970), p. 310.
16. Op. cit., pars. 283–84.

become public figures. He felt that what people would be interested in hearing was not explanations of what departments were doing but what permanent secretaries themselves thought and what advice they were giving to ministers. For that reason, he felt it would be very difficult for permanent secretaries to make public speeches. They would either be forced to be boring or tempted to be indiscreet.[17]

Desmond Roche commented on the situation in the Irish civil service:

The traditional attitude has been to present as narrow a front as possible towards the public, since from that direction there is little to be expected except mud and brickbats. Consequently information is strictly controlled or channelled—sometimes to the point of ceasing to flow at all. It requires an effort to change so well established a position, which has on the whole been advantageous to the defenders.[18]

The Civil Service Regulation Act 1956

This Act makes provision for the regulation, control and management of the civil service. Section 5 provides that every established civil servant holds office at the will and pleasure of the government. What this means is that only the government is empowered to dispense with the services of an established civil servant; the government may do this at any time without any form of notice, and in fact, the terms of employment of civil servants are not subject to legal enforcement. In practice, however, this power is used very rarely and then only for very grave reason involving serious misconduct.

Indeed, it is understood that there is doubt about the legal right of a civil servant to his salary and whether he can succeed in a suit for arrears of pay due to him. In practice, there is rarely litigation over dismissals since they seldom occur. It has been said that "The British civil servant's tenure is legally the most insecure in the world,

---

17. James Dunnett, "Equipping the Civil Service for its Tasks", *Public Administration*, XLVII, 1 (1969), 13–31.

18. Desmond Roche, "The Civil Servant and Public Relations", *Administration*, XI, 2 (1963), 108.

but in practice it is the most secure",[19] and this holds true of Irish civil servants as well.

William Smyth refers to the part played by personnel managers in the disciplinary area:

> . . . the integrity and loyalty of civil servants are so well established as to be taken virtually for granted. The more drastic range of penalties provided in the disciplinary code is very rarely invoked; in effect, it is largely a reserved power. Public personnel managers are attuned to a more positive and more developmental role. They stress the great dynamic for socio-economic progress which the public service contains. They are concerned to provide the organisational climates and structures which are most conducive to the release of that dynamic. They are concerned to avoid the incalculable cost arising from the underuse or misuse of human talents. These are matters of much greater moment than reinforcing a disciplinary code or the diligent pursuit of the few who fall from grace.[20]

Section 6 of the 1956 Act provides that civil servants who are not established may have their services terminated by what the Act terms "the appropriate authority", which, in practice, means the minister in charge of the department or office where the officer is serving.

Equally, the "appropriate authority" may terminate the services of a civil servant who has been appointed to an established position, if a condition of that appointment is that he serve a period of probation and if during that period he fails to fulfil the conditions attaching to the probation. Generally these conditions are that his performance of duty, conduct and health are satisfactory.

Section 8 provides that the retiring age is sixty-five years and that every civil servant must retire on reaching that age. It also provides that the "appropriate authority" may require an officer to retire when he has reached the age of sixty. The section also states

19.   Bernard Schwartz and H. W. R. Wade, *Legal Control of Government: Administrative Law in Britain and the United States* (Oxford: Clarendon Press, 1972), pp. 24–25.
20.   William Smyth, "The Responsibility of the Civil Servant in Ireland", *Administration*, XXIII, 4 (1975), 358.

that in certain circumstances the retiring age may be extended, under conditions prescribed from time to time by the Minister for the Public Service. In general these conditions relate to cases of hardship and have been referred to in chapter 6. The only circumstance in which an established civil servant (other than an officer on probation) can be removed from office without the approval of the government is where his retirement is effected on the grounds of ill health. Section 9 of the Act authorises such retirement subject to stringent conditions, including the officer's right to appeal to a medical referee against a minister's decision that he is permanently incapacitated on health grounds.

The Act contains a number of provisions relating to civil service discipline. Section 13 enables a minister (or a civil servant nominated by him) to suspend an officer of his department where (i) it appears that the officer has been guilty of grave misconduct or of grave irregularity warranting disciplinary action, (ii) where it appears that the public interest might be prejudiced by allowing the officer to remain on duty or (iii) where a charge of grave misconduct or irregularity has been made against the officer which appears to warrant investigation. An officer receives no pay while under suspension. If the suspension is lifted, the pay may be restored in whole or in part at the discretion of the minister.

Section 15 authorises reductions in pay and reductions in grade, the power of decision being vested in the minister in charge of the officer's department. If there is a loss of public moneys, the decision ordinarily rests with the Minister for the Public Service, though he is authorised to delegate this function to the individual minister.

Perhaps the most common form of disciplinary action against a civil servant is the deferment or withholding of an annual salary increment. Increments are, as already mentioned, granted only where the head of the department or office concerned is satisfied with the officer's service and the decision to withhold or defer an increment is, therefore, within the competence of the head.

Every civil servant is entitled to appeal to his minister against a disciplinary decision. This right, while non-statutory, is firmly enshrined in practice. Indeed, in general the law is a poor guide to an understanding of the position of the civil servant in society, his duties, rights and responsibilities. These are largely defined by current interpretations of written and unwritten conventions or 'practices' accumulated and evolved through the years.

The Act confers upon the Minister for the Public Service various powers in relation to the civil service. These powers include (i) the regulation and control of the civil service, (ii) the classification, numbers and remuneration of civil servants, and (iii) the fixing of terms and conditions of service, including the conditions governing promotion. Under this provision, the Minister for the Public Service may make such arrangements, which in practice cover a wide and varied range of matters, as he thinks fit.

The Department of the Public Service

The Department of the Public Service was established in November 1973 following the passing of the Ministers and Secretaries (Amendment) Act 1973.[21] In his speech on the second reading of the bill, the Minister for Finance said: "The establishment of this Department is an essential step in the implementation of the recommendations of the Public Services Organisation Review Group."[22] In fact the group had specifically recommended the setting up of the new department:

We recommend . . . that the central organisation and personnel functions for the public service should be removed from the Department of Finance and assigned to a new Department. The reorganisation of the public service should be the responsibility of this Department which we call the Public Service Department.[23]

On the establishment of the new department, most of the powers relating to public servants, which had been exercised by the Minister for Finance, were transferred to the Minister for the Public Service by the Public Service (Transfer of Departmental Administration and Ministerial Functions) Order 1973.[24] The powers referred to had been previously exercised by a division in the Department of Finance

---

21.   Ministers and Secretaries (Amendment) Act 1973 (no. 14).
22.   *Dáil Debates,* Vol. 267, 3 July 1973, Col. 51.
23.   Par. 14.4.1.
24.   S.I. No. 294.

originally termed the establishments division but more recently re-named the personnel division. In his speech the Minister for Finance explained why the transfer was being made:

The case for the assignment of these functions together with responsibility for the coordination of organisation and personnel matters for the whole public service to a separate Department of the Public Service is based on a few fundamental considerations. In the first place, the review group found that, in the past, these functions have tended to be subordinated to the financial and economic responsibilities of the Department of Finance; secondly, the skills employed by the organisation and personnel functions are so different from those required by the finance and planning functions that they should be under a separate permanent Departmental head and, thirdly, it is essential that the organisation and personnel functions for the public sector should be given the status they have acquired in the private sector. The eventual assignment to the Department of the Public Service of responsibility for the coordination of all public service organisation and personnel practices is a logical consequence of the acceptance of the idea of a unified public service.

The Minister went on to say:

I would like to give a brief outline of how I foresee the operation of the new Department. Its first task will be to equip itself for the renewal of the public service. As the central unit of service-wide systems of organisation and personnel, it must first of all ensure that the levels of skill it possesses and which are possessed by the organisation and personnel units in all Departments are equal to the best available. Secondly, it must press on with the reorganisation of the public service on a fundamental basis on lines like those suggested in the report of the review group. Finally, it must guide and coordinate the general structural changes required to produce a public service combining unity of purpose and efficient and effective deployment of resources with diversity of initiative towards the attainment of national goals.

The new department has three divisions—personnel, remuneration and organisation—each of which is headed by a deputy secretary. The work of these divisions, as presented by the deputy
secretaries in papers to the Public Service Advisory Council, is summarised in the appendix to the Council's first report.[25] This Council
was set up in accordance with a recommendation of the Devlin
report:

> The reorganisation of the public service and its subsequent
> maintenance at the highest possible level of efficiency is a matter
> of such great public interest that it must be subject to a dynamic
> for adaptation from outside and it must be seen to be contin-
> uously adapting itself. We, therefore, recommend the establish-
> ment of a Public Service Advisory Council of eight persons—
> four from the private sector, three from the public sector and
> the Secretary of the Public Service Department,—to survey the
> progress of the reorganisation of the public service. . . . The
> Advisory Council should review the work of the Department
> and its progress in the reorganisation of the public service in a
> report presented to the Minister for Finance and the Public
> Service each year. This report, after consideration by the Gov-
> ernment, should be laid before the Oireachtas. . . . It should be
> able to suggest new methods and techniques but should not
> have executive powers. Its members should be nominated by
> the Government and, to secure an incentive for change from
> outside the public service, the Chairman should also be nom-
> inated by the Government from the private sector represen-
> tatives.[26]

Personnel Division

This division has four sections: recruitment, general matters, manpower development and training.

The recruitment section deals with the various aspects of recruitment to the civil service, including manpower forecasting and planning, as well as the adaptation of recruitment procedures. It also

---

25. *Public Service Advisory Council Report for Year ended 31 October 1974*
    (Dublin: Stationery Office, 1975), Prl. 4509.
26. Par. 14.1.6.

deals with recruitment to institutions of the European Community and with the decentralisation of government departments. The director of recruitment is a civil service commissioner and the section cooperates closely with the Civil Service Commission.

The general section is responsible for the general regulations affecting the civil service in matters other than those of pay. For example, it deals with questions relating to aspects of sick, annual or special leave; with ensuring the implementation of the recommendations of the Commission on the Status of Women relating to the position of women in state employment; with the introduction of flexible working hours and other miscellaneous matters.

The manpower development section deals with matters concerning promotion, further education (other than training), staff reporting and appraisal, and information systems.

The training section coordinates and organises training for civil servants and assesses training needs, as well as undertaking the establishment of a service-wide programme of staff development. It works in close liaison with the Institute of Public Administration, one of whose functions is the provision of training for the entire public service.

Remuneration Division

This division also has four sections and, in addition, provides the secretariat for the Review Body on Higher Remuneration in the Public Sector.

The first section is concerned with the operation of conciliation and arbitration schemes for the civil service and for advisory staff of the county committees of agriculture. It is also concerned with the application of national pay rounds to the civil service and deals with general problems of industrial relations which affect the public service. It is the expressed aim of this section, in consultation with staff interests, to rationalise the present arrangements under which many different arbitration boards exist for the public service.

The second section is concerned, in the context of the public sector, with the Employer/Labour Conference (including the negotiation of national pay agreements), general pay questions (including pay coordination within the sector), matters related to pay in state-sponsored bodies and the remuneration aspects of an incomes policy.

The third section is concerned with arrangements for the pay of higher civil servants, parliamentarians, the judiciary, state solicitors, sub-postmasters, employment exchange managers and industrial civil servants and with pay and allowances for gardaí, army and teachers; servicing of the joint industrial council for industrial civil servants; determination of rates of pay for new posts; non-capital pay estimates; long-term pay forecasting; fixing of fees, gratuities and allowances.

The fourth section is concerned with the various superannuation schemes for the entire public sector, including groups such as the judiciary, parliamentarians and the staffs of state-sponsored bodies.

Organisation Division

This division has five sections and in addition provides the secretariat for the Public Service Advisory Council.

The staff gradings and numbers section is responsible for overall control and authorisation of new posts with appropriate gradings within the civil service.

The structures section is concerned with the machinery of government and the structural development of the public service, and, amongst other things, with giving effect to the concepts and recommendations contained in the Devlin report relating to the public service structures of the future.

The management services section is responsible for matters relating to the internal managerial efficiency of the civil service and certain related public service agencies. It promotes, develops and employs organisation and methods, work survey and general management techniques in departments and, where appropriate, in related state-sponsored bodies.

The central data processing section is responsible for the formulation of policy for electronic data processing development in the civil service and certain related public service agencies, the co-ordination and determination of the overall computer hardware requirements and the development of computer systems; operation and development of a computer bureau for the civil service and related public service agencies; general data processing matters and overall management information systems; and national policy issues regarding overall computer development.

The operations research section is concerned with promoting and using operations research and related management science techniques and methods as an aid to decision-making in government departments and in related state-sponsored bodies.

The Minister for the Public Service is also the Minister for Finance, as was recommended by the Public Service Organisation Review Body:

Organisation and personnel cannot easily be divorced from the budgetary function; each function is concerned with the deployment of manpower, the principal resource of all organisa-tions, but it is essential that organisation and personnel have their own voice to the Minister. When the three functions are combined in a single Department, the budgetary function inevitably takes precedence; the urgent financial business must get first attention.[27]

---

27.   Par. 14.1.2.

Chapter Nine

The Future

It seems reasonably certain, unless there is a marked change in people's attitudes towards the part to be played by the state in the progress of national development, that it will be required to continue to expand its activities in various fields, such as health, housing, education, culture and the environment. To achieve this growth, continued attention will have to be paid to the institutions required to advise government and to give effect to its decisions, and, in particular, to the organisation and staffing of these institutions. The Public Service Advisory Council has pointed to the need for improving the cost effectiveness of the public service generally. It attaches the highest importance to the development of a work programme designed to determine the most effective means (by reference to structures, organisation, staffing and programme content) of achieving desirable objectives and to isolate areas in which the costs of public service organisations or activities should be questioned in terms of the benefits which flow from them. The objective of the programme would be to achieve the optimum quality of public service to the nation, having regard to the total cost which the nation is willing to pay.[1] Some of the issues likely to arise have been identified in the Devlin report; others are being brought to notice by official statements and in public debate arising from changes in social attitudes to employment.

The first intimation of the government's intention to establish a review body (the Devlin committee) came from the Minister for Finance in his budget speech on 9 March 1966, a month after the appointment of the Fulton Committee in Britain:

The Civil Service has shown a remarkable capacity to adapt

---

1. *Public Service Advisory Council Report for Year ended 31 October 1974,* par. 5.1.3.

itself to new functions and has been doing its work with great skill, devotion and integrity. Its good qualities are founded on the statutory requirement of open competitive recruitment. At this stage in the evolution of national policies, when the Service faces responsibilities and tasks going far beyond the earlier concepts of administration, and Departments are expected to become more active agencies of development, it seems timely to arrange for a review of the existing organisation at administrative level.

It is a long time since any general look was taken at how the Civil Service is functioning in a changing world. Every organisation can benefit from periodic review. If a review of this kind is to be done well, it will take time. Its procedure must be flexible. Close contact must be maintained with both management and staff concerned. A blend of experience of high quality of the working of both the public service and of business will help to make it apt and effective. It would to my mind best be conducted by a special group combining representatives of the business and professional world and persons no longer serving who have had broad experience in the Civil Service and in State enterprises. I hope to assemble such a group during the coming months.[2]

By September 1966, the chairman, Mr Liam St. J. Devlin, and the other members of the group had been assembled, with the following mandate, already quoted in chapter one:

Having regard to the growing responsibilities of Government, to examine and report on the organisation of the Departments of State at the higher levels, including the appropriate distribution of functions as between both Departments themselves and Departments and other bodies.

The group's report raised a number of issues which are already occupying, and will continue to occupy, the time and energies of both management and staff in the civil service. The implementation

2. *Dáil Debates*, Vol. 221, 9 March 1966, Cols. 1306–07.

of the various recommendations will affect both the nature and style of the work at present being carried out by civil servants. Some of these recommendations—and not necessarily the most important in the eyes of ministers, politicians, management, staff and staff associations—will now be considered briefly.

Separation of the Making of Policy from its Execution

In referring to the growing responsibilities of government in the social, economic and cultural fields and to the likelihood that these will increase further, the Devlin group emphasised the need for the choice of the best policies for progress, consistent with the maintenance of the essential freedoms and the efficient management of the everyday business of government. It pointed out that under the existing system of departments, where the minister, as a corporation sole under the Ministers and Secretaries Acts, is responsible for every executive act of his department, the senior staff are, of necessity, so occupied with the pressure of day-to-day business that they have little time to take part in the formulation of the overall policy of their department's functional areas. The problem, as the group saw it, was how to free these officials from the day-to-day execution of policy and simultaneously create effective reporting and communication systems between those responsible for the execution of settled policy and those whose concern is the determination and review of policy. This was the point made earlier by T. K. Whitaker when he wrote:

I am not sure now if the biggest problem after all will not be one of organisation—how Secretaries and other senior officers can organise their time and work so as to get away from their desks and the harrassing experiences of everyday sufficiently to read, consider and consult with others in order to be able to give sound and comprehensive advice on future development policy.[3]

The group's proposals for remedying the defects in the system were based on the concept of a number of centres, each of which would consist of a minister and his closest advisers concerned with policy, overall direction and control of his department's activities.

---

3. T. K. Whitaker, "The Civil Service and Development", *Administration*, IX, 2 (1961), 87.

Each centre would be surrounded by a number of units which would perform the executive work at present carried out by departments, by commissions, and by the non-commercial state-sponsored bodies. The central core would be called the *aireacht* and the units would comprise the executive area. The essence of the model put forward is that the public service has two main roles: (i) advising the government on policy, examining and suggesting various lines of action, and reviewing for the government the operation of existing policies, and (ii) the detailed execution of settled policy.

Within the *aireacht*, the concept of the minister as a corporation sole would continue to apply: the actions of the staff would remain the actions of the minister. (The term 'corporation sole' derives from section 2 (1) of the Ministers and Secretaries Act 1924 which specified that "Each of the ministers mentioned in section 1 shall be a corporation sole under his style or name aforesaid. . . . " The Devlin report noted that "The effect of the statutory provisions is that the acts of a Department are the acts of its Minister. Unless there is a statutory exception no civil servant can, in law, give a decision.")[4] The Devlin group proposed a change in the structure of departments so that the actions of the officials in the executive area would not be the actions of the minister and the 'corporation sole' concept would not apply in that area.

The group foresaw the public service of the future as consisting of a number of departments, each divided into an *aireacht* and executive units. The units would comprise executive offices (units which would discharge executive functions now carried out by departments) and executive agencies (units which would discharge their executive functions, under the general supervision of part-time boards, on the lines of the existing non-commercial state-sponsored bodies).

The business of the staff of each *aireacht*, as stated by the group, would be:

(i) The formulation of overall strategy, the general policy of the Department and the preparation of legislation. This will be done through the co-ordination by the Secretary of

---

4. Op. cit., par. 4.1.9.

alternative policy proposals which he will submit, with his recommendations as to choice, for decision by the Minister.

(ii) The co-ordination and continuous appraisal and review of existing policies in regard to the executive responsibilities of the Department.

(iii) With the transfer of executive activities from the Aireacht, it is essential that there should be a feedback to the Aireacht of the cases where the execution of policy is causing difficulties. This is an input to the process of appraisal.

(iv) General direction and control of the executive activities of the Department. By this we mean the need to be satisfied that the discharge of these activities is efficiently organised and managed. There should be no interference in day-to-day management as this would detract from the executive responsibility of unit heads.

(v) International activities of the Department.[5]

The group went on to say that to enable him carry out this business, the secretary should have four staff functions reporting to him: the units for finance, planning, organisation and personnel.

The government accepted the group's recommendation to establish such a system and decided that it should be put into operation on an experimental basis. Accordingly, five departments were chosen for the experiment (Health, Transport and Power, Industry and Commerce, Local Government and Defence) and a study of each department was undertaken by a team of officials representing the particular department and the Department of the Public Service. As a result, restructuring proposals for two of the departments were accepted by the government and were published.[6] At the time of writing, the results of the study of the other departments have not been made known.

The suggested system bears some resemblance to that obtaining in Sweden. A basic characteristic of the Swedish civil service is that it is organised at two separate levels—ministries and agencies. The former are primarily responsible for the framing of policy and the

---

5.   ibid., par. 13.2.1.
6.   *Restructuring the Department of Health: The Separation of Policy and Execution* (Dublin: Stationery Office, 1973), Prl. 3445.

latter principally for its execution. In his interesting account of how the system works, Pierre Vinde includes the following remarks about the staffing of these bodies:

> Service in the ministries is as a rule of limited duration. . . . It is considered that the majority of civil servants should leave the ministries by the age of forty to forty-five. They should rarely stay beyond fifty. The reasons advanced for this procedure include the following: The conditions of service, i.e. pace of work and working hours, are such that it is not reasonable to expect persons over forty to forty-five to stand them. The versatility of mind and the energy of people aged thirty-five to forty-five make them ideal for policy-shaping positions. After this their experience can be more fruitfully employed in leading positions in the agencies. Practically all Directors-General, most Assistant Directors-General and a large number of Heads of Department and Division are appointed from among senior ministerial officials.[7]

One of the deputy secretaries of the Department of the Public Service had this to say about the *aireacht* experiment:

> One of the critical questions . . . is . . . why should we experiment with the notion rather than go ahead and implement it immediately? This has been commented on in public on more than one occasion—sometimes adversely. So it is important that we be clear on why we are experimenting and on what we mean by an experiment. We are experimenting because the essence of the Aireacht concept is that it requires a new emphasis in the role and functioning of Ministers and their interaction with Parliament. For instance the notion of 'corporation sole' as it applies to Ministers will undergo a radical change if the Aireacht concept is applied permanently. The fundamental issues here are so far-reaching that Parliament and Government, naturally, wish to see the implications of the new situation in physical terms before statutory commitment is given to them. Experimentation is a very real first step towards development of the Aireacht concept, not a recipe for procrastination.

---

7.   Pierre Vinde, "An Introduction to the Swedish Civil Service", *Administration*, XVI, 2 (1968), 105.

What do we mean by an experiment? What we are doing in relation to the Departments I have mentioned is restructuring them, physically, on Aireacht/Executive Unit lines and having them operate in accordance with the Aireacht concept for a stated period. During this period the practicability, parliamentary/governmental acceptance and general value of the Aireacht concept will be appraised and evaluated for its effectiveness and usefulness in the context of Irish Governmental and Public Service operations. At the end of the period the Government will be asked to decide whether or not the Aireacht concept should be one of the permanent features of our public service. Let us be clear however on the fact that during the experiment it is intended that Departments will be physically restructured on Aireacht lines and will operate accordingly. You will appreciate from what I have said earlier in relation to the dimensions to reform, that Parliament, Government and various other groups have a vital concern in the essentials of the Aireacht concept.

I believe that the purist notion of an Aireacht as outlined in the report of the Public Services Organisation Review Group, while certainly a model to be aimed for, is also one which, in the light of reality, may need to be modified to meet different circumstances in different portfolio areas. For instance, in today's circumstances operational or executive aspects of the administration of justice in Ireland are highly sensitive and thus of more direct concern to the Minister involved and to Government than they might be, say, ten or twenty years hence. So as I see it the Aireacht and its related structures and procedures must be regarded in a flexible fashion. Also, the linking of it to appellate machinery is highly important in order to preserve the best interests of democracy.[8]

Staff Units for Planning, Finance, Organisation and Personnel

In his budget speech of 1970, the Minister for Finance said:

The central feature of the [Devlin] report concerns the arrangements for the overall organisation and management of the

---

8.   Noel Whelan, "Reform (or Change) in the Irish Public Service 1969–1975". An address to the Institute of Public Administration, 2 October 1975.

public service through the functions of planning, finance, organisation and personnel. The Government have decided, in
accordance with the group's recommendation, to establish in
Departments specialised staff units for these functions, separate
from the executive functions of Departments. A first task of
these units will be to examine systematically the executive operations so as to produce the most efficient allocation of responsibilities. The guidelines for each Department contained in the
report will provide an excellent starting point for this examination.[9]

In accordance with this decision, arrangements are proceeding
for establishing these four coordinating and managerial functions in
all departments. They have been installed already in the Department
of Health and the intention is to introduce them in other departments as they, too, are restructured. The purpose of the staff units
would be to assist the secretary of the department, as head of the
aireacht, in carrying out its business.

Outline position descriptions have been provided for the heads
of each of the four units—in the case of the Department of Health,
the duties of the head of each unit, within the authority delegated
by the secretary of the department, have been defined as follows:

Planning: to advise and assist line management in the planning
and evaluation of services, to provide analytical information and
capacity for the policy-forming areas of the health services, and
to assist the development of the planning and evaluation function in the executive area.

Finance: to advise and assist line management in linking service
planning and execution to budgeting, in controlling expenditure
within budgets, and in seeking effectiveness and efficiency in the
utilisation of financial resources.

Organisation: to assist and advise line management, in association with the other staff functions, particularly the personnel
unit, to secure the best disposition of people, systems and processes in the health services administration.

---

9.   *Dáil Debates*, Vol. 245, 22 April 1970, Col. 1750.

Personnel: to assist and advise line management, in association with the other staff functions, particularly the organisation unit, in ensuring the provision, training and development of adequate staff for the provision of the health services and to monitor, negotiate on and review, as required, the remuneration and conditions of service of staffs employed in the health services.[10]

The Devlin report recommended the establishment of similar staff units in all the major executive agencies as well as in the central departments. The group saw these as being the common functions which run through all the separate parts of the public service to provide a coordinating system and to produce a unity of purpose out of the diversity of effort. Through these functions, they held that essential communications could be maintained throughout the public service and the overall coordination of the service secured.[11]

In the paper to which reference has already been made, the deputy secretary of the Department of the Public Service described the four functions as critical for effective and efficient management within the total public sector. Each of these functions requires a range of specialist skills which are at present very much under-developed (in some cases non-existent) within the civil service and a great deal of work will have to be done to ensure that staff attain these skills in future. "If one could visualise a situation where these four staff functions are highly developed as between various government departments and indeed other public service agencies it is apparent that mobility, a highly desirable requirement, could be enhanced throughout the public service." Noel Whelan went on to say that the two central departments—Public Service and Finance—have been the subject of detailed analysis in order to restructure them on lines compatible with their central responsibilities for organisation and personnel (in the case of the Department of the Public Service) and finance and planning (in the case of the Department of Finance).

The Department of the Public Service is already structured and organised on the basis of its two central functions. Work is very

---

10. *Restructuring the Department of Health*, pp. 62–65.
11. Op. cit., par. 12.4.1.

far advanced in relation to the similar restructuring of the Department of Finance.

Appellate Procedures

Because the activities of public bodies affect so many aspects of the individual citizen's life, it is inevitable that he should feel that these bodies occasionally infringe on his constitutional or legal rights. He may occasionally be dissatisfied with the procedures they have followed, he may believe that benefits to which he is entitled have not been given to him, or he may feel that he has been unfairly treated. Sometimes the complaint is that there has been undue delay in arriving at a decision.

It is part of every administrative system to have some means by which the grievances of the citizen against public bodies can be considered and, if well-founded, remedied. These systems of review can be formal or informal. In Ireland the formal system includes action in the High Court and Supreme Court, where constitutional and legal rights are concerned, and, more generally, appeals to ministers and to administrative tribunals. The informal systems include approaches to parliamentary representatives, to interest groups and to trade unions, as well as correspondence and publicity in the press. Generally, the citizens' grievances can be classified under the headings of constitutional rights, legal rights, failure to follow correct procedures, unfairness in arriving at a decision, a mistaken view of the facts, unreasonable exercise of discretion in relation to the facts, as well as delay or failure in reaching a decision.

Dealing with grievances of this kind is a major feature of the systems of public administration in a number of countries where a great deal has been done to establish formal systems for considering and remedying the grievances of the citizen against the administration. The position in Ireland is much less developed. Nonetheless, three distinct systems can be seen at work—the judicial system through the courts, the administrative system through administrative tribunals of one kind or another, and the parliamentary system through ministers and public representatives. Usually recourse will be had to the courts, when the appellant considers that the action taken by the administrative agency is within the law but contrary to his constitutional rights, or is outside or against the provisions of the law, or if he feels that the procedure adopted is defective. Since the court procedure is slow and expensive, it is usually adopted only in important matters or after other remedies have been exhausted.

A great volume of the grievances of the individual citizen is dealt with through administrative tribunals: the special commissioners of income tax, the appeals officers of the Department of Social Welfare, the Redundancy Appeals Tribunal are examples. Here the procedure is usually speedy, informal and inexpensive. In some cases no formal tribunal at the official level exists, but there is a legal right of appeal to a minister. He usually requests that an inquiry of some kind be held and then, having considered what has been adduced, gives a decision. The most notable example of this type of procedure is the right of appeal by citizens to the Minister for Local Government against decisions by local authorities, especially in relation to town-planning decisions, proposals for compulsory acquisition of land, and so on. The normal position here is that the law provides for this appeal, that the decision of the minister on a question of fact is final, but that there may be an appeal to the courts on points of law. Within the law, therefore, ministers are not normally accountable to the courts for the decisions taken, but to the Dáil. This procedure is a half-way house between a system of administrative tribunals and the parliamentary system.

The third main procedure adopted in Ireland is the fully parliamentary system whereby a public representative, usually a Dáil deputy, gets in touch informally with the appropriate minister, or formally asks a question about the matter in the Dáil. If he believes the matter to be sufficiently grave, he can raise the matter by way of a formal motion in the House.

In general the Irish system provides ministers and their civil servants with a wide degree of discretion in arriving at a decision. The courts will not normally interfere with any such decision provided that constitutional rights, the terms of the relative legislation and correct procedures have been followed. Similarly, where a ministerial decision has been raised in parliament and the minister is prepared to defend it, it is unlikely that there will be parliamentary intervention to get the decision altered. This is not so in a number of other countries where regular systems of administrative courts exist, to which the citizen can appeal on questions of law, on questions of fact and also on whether discretion has been reasonably exercised. This is the system of the *conseil d'état.*

In a number of countries, also, parliament has its own system for inquiring into the methods by which ministerial and official decisions have been made. This is the institution of the ombudsman. Generally, although the volume of appeals in a modern state which go to a *conseil d'état* or to administrative tribunals is enormous, the number of cases where maladministration is alleged through the parliamentary process and referred to the ombudsman, or taken up by him on his own initiative, is quite small.

The Devlin group regarded the question of administrative justice and appellate procedures as an integral part of its study and therefore included as an appendix to its report a note on this subject which was prepared by a working party under the aegis of the Institute of Public Administration. The chairman of the working party was the then Chief Justice, the Honourable Cearbhall Ó Dálaigh, now President of Ireland. The working party adverted to the multitude of decisions taken daily by civil servants in every department without reference to the minister but for which the minister was nevertheless responsible in law. It also drew attention to the main group's suggestion that in the future many of these decisions should be taken by officers in executive agencies, for which decisions ministers would no longer be responsible.

> The steady growth in the functions of government, the increasing extent to which they impinge on the citizen, the growth of a closer sense of community and the place of fair dealing in that community, the growth of a greater sense of self-assertion by the citizen, and the extent to which governmental actions can be facilitated if the citizens are assured that they will be treated fairly—all these enhance the need for adequate appellate institutions and procedures. This need would be made the more urgent on any assumption that implementing work be hived off from Ministers to executive agencies of some sort, so removing much of the existing remedies through Ministers. As one consequence it would be necessary to have some effective 'feedback' to the Ministry to show how policies worked in practice. But the

main need would be to make sure that the citizen was adequately protected against injustice or neglect.[12]

The working party consequently recommended that an appeal tribunal should be set up in every major executive agency and that, where the volume of work would not justify a separate tribunal for each agency, a tribunal for a group of small agencies might be attached to the parent ministry. To ensure that the tribunals were working well, to establish new ones where necessary and, in the last resort, to invoke the process of judicial review, the working party recommended the appointment of a Commissioner for Administrative Justice. This officer would advise on aspects of administrative law in relation to existing legislation and also perform the functions of an ombudsman in following up complaints from the public in cases where no tribunal existed or where administrative remedies had been exhausted. The working party felt that the Commissioner would have all the powers of an ombudsman while at the same time having a general administrative competence in relation to tribunals.

In January 1975 the Minister for the Public Service had this to say on the subject:

> Of great importance both to the public and to the public service itself is the question of administrative justice. I am anxious to ensure the availability of means of appeal to the citizen who feels aggrieved by the actions of public servants. Such an appeals system would help to prove what every experienced citizen knows to be true, that our public servants invariably act with total integrity and objectivity. Nevertheless, human nature not being perfect, mistakes can arise and it is desirable that there should be a means of correcting them. This is an important and difficult area of administration and its examination with a view to producing solutions suitable to Irish conditions is proceeding in my Department.[13]

---

12. *Report of Public Services Organisation Review Group 1966–1969*, Appendix 1, "Note on Administrative Law and Procedure", par. 3.4.
13. "Privileged to be in the Public Service". An address to the Galway Chamber of Commerce, 25 January 1975.

Later that year when speaking in Dáil Eireann on the motion (which was agreed) "That Dáil Eireann favours the appointment of an Ombudsman", the minister went further:

Departments of State and public authorities are probably not the best judges of their own conduct. It is probably a healthy thing to have their conduct looked at by some independent authority. Life is becoming more complex. Citizens, individually and collectively, are becoming more dependent on the State, not because the State as an entity has sought to get extra powers for itself, but because society has called on the community through the State to provide welfare services, health services, educational services; because society has obliged the State to protect the public good with rules for physical planning, because the community has conferred upon the public authority rights of compulsory purchase in the public interest. In the exercise of these duties and obligations the State must make judgments from time to time about the eligibility of people for certain benefits which are available. It must also pass judgment on where the balance should be struck between the private interest and the common good.

This is an area in which tremendous good can be done. In most cases, decisions are taken which are for the benefit of the community. If some decision is taken to confer benefit on the community, there are ways and means of ensuring that an individual is not harmed as a consequence. Because of the multitude of decisions and the immense complexity of ways and means of conferring or withholding benefit, it is possible that human error will result in perfection not being achieved at all times. It is clearly necessary to have some system which will reconcile the necessary exercise of governmental authority with the interests of the individual. . . . The Government have given some thought to this matter and there are a number of possibilities. We could produce our own legislation and seek the approval of the Dáil and Seanad Eireann for that, but it would be preferable to have an all-party committee of the Oireachtas, an informal committee which would work fairly quickly to consider all aspects of the matter.[14]

14. *Dáil Debates*, Vol. 280, No. 8, 7 May 1975, Cols. 1374–81.

In December 1975 the minister announced the formation of such a committee, consisting of ten members of the Dáil, with himself as chairman, to find "a cheap, informal and expeditious means of having grievances examined by an impartial authority."[15]

The appointment of an ombudsman will no doubt be a matter of considerable interest to civil servants. When the Whyatt committee was considering the question of the appointment of an ombudsman in Britain, one of the arguments put to it against such an appointment was that civil servants would not be able to do their work properly with the threat of an outside investigation hanging over them—that they would be even more frightened of making decisions.

The committee pointed out that these were the same fears which had been expressed by civil servants in Denmark when the appointment of a parliamentary commissioner was being discussed there. As it turned out, they had not been realised. On the contrary, the Danish ombudsman had come to be regarded by civil servants as a valuable and impartial defence against unjustified criticism to which the individual civil servant could not himself respond, and had fostered a feeling of confidence between civil servants and members of the public. "The Parliamentary Commissioner should . . . be regarded neither as simply the 'watchdog' of the public nor the apologist of the administration, but as the independent upholder of the highest standards of efficient and fair administration."[16]

The committee pointed out that one of the ombudsman's powers and duties had an important bearing on this point. If he received a series of complaints and found that they were due to stupid or unjust regulations which civil servants had to administer, perhaps against their will, he could draw the attention of parliament to these regulations and ask for their amendment.

The views of the Whyatt committee were supported by Nordskov Nielsen, the Danish ombudsman, in an address given to a public meeting in Dublin on 30 May 1972:

Another objection is that the Ombudsman's way of operating

---

15. *The Irish Times*, 15 December 1975.
16. *A Report by Justice. The Citizen and the Administration: The Redress of Grievances* (London: Stevens and Sons Limited, 1961), par. 162.

may destroy confidence in the administration. When the Ombudsman institution was being set up in Denmark, it was feared that it would create a popular atmosphere of distrust of public personnel, of their work methods, and so forth. I am convinced that this fear has been unfounded. I daresay even that the Ombudsman institution has meant a strengthening of the administration's reputation among ordinary people. The reasons are several. Due to the treatment of the administration by the press one might have been led to believe that there was much corruption and grave neglect of office. The results of the Ombudsman's work have removed this error of prejudice, or of ignorance. The number of serious cases of proven corruption or neglect of office are extremely low. I believe it has made an impression that the total number of complaints submitted to the Ombudsman are relatively few. More fundamental and interesting in my opinion is the viewpoint that confidence in the administration is deepened and enhanced in proportion as it is open to the public view and is firmly within the control and supervision of an outside authority. It is lack of publicity and lack of control which—rightly—creates distrust and rumour.[17]

Revision of the Grading System

Many people who have written on the role of civil servants in administration have referred to the relationship between the professional and the administrator because of the general impression, confirmed by some evidence, that the present situation leads to frustration, a waste of resources and immobility.[18] The Devlin and

17. Nordskov Nielsen, "The Danish Ombudsman", *Administration*, XXI, 3 (1973), 364.
18. R. G. S. Brown, *The Administrative Process in Britain*, chapter 13, "The Generalist in Public Administration".
   John Garrett, *The Management of Government* (Harmondsworth: Penguin Books, 1972), chapter 2, "Fulton: The Establishment, The System, The Amateur".
   F. Ridley (ed.), *Specialists and Generalists: A Comparative Study of the Professional Civil Servant at Home and Abroad* (London: George Allen and Unwin Ltd., 1968).
   V. Subramaniam, "The Relative Status of Specialists and Generalists", *Public Administration*, XLVI, 3 (1968), 331–40.
   T. K. Whitaker, "The Administrator and the Professional in the Irish Public Service", *Léargas* (a monthly review of public affairs published by the Institute of Public Administration, Dublin, February/March 1966, 4–7).

Fulton reports contained comment and recommendations on this issue. The Devlin report refers to the problem of the "Administrator and the Professional" or the "Dual Structure",[19] while the Fulton report refers to the "manifest disadvantages" which arise from organising specialists into separate hierarchies and reserving the policy and financial aspects of their work to generalists.[20] The former came to the conclusion that there were two separate problems—one of organisation and one of personnel—and that the personnel problem was an emotive subject which tended to obscure the real facts of the case. The report set out these problems thus:

> Organisationally, there is the problem of the dual structure, the fact that two parallel hierarchies exist side by side for the performance of a single function. Schematically, the dual structure is as follows:

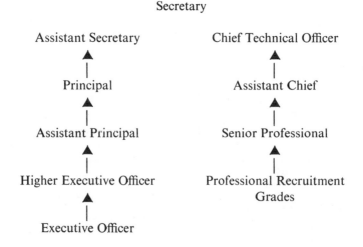

Secretary

Assistant Secretary   Chief Technical Officer

Principal   Assistant Chief

Assistant Principal   Senior Professional

Higher Executive Officer   Professional Recruitment
                               Grades

Executive Officer

> When such a professional or technical structure is advisory or inspectorial, the main complaint of the professional officer is that he is asked for advice which may be accepted or rejected

19. Op. cit., par. 10.11.4.
20. Op. cit., par. 38.

by the general service side. When the structure is engaged on executive work, the organisation is inherently cumbersome. The professional structure is responsible for the formulation and carrying out of projects; the generalist structure is responsible for overall policy, the approval of individual schemes from the financial aspect and for general administration of schemes. While the higher professional staff have a managerial role, approval of staffing quotas and of items of expenditure, including travelling, is the responsibility of the generalist structure. Strictly on organisation, proposals should flow up the professional structure and be submitted by the Chief Technical Officer to his opposite number, the head of the generalist structure. The latter should submit the proposal down the line to his staff who should examine it from the aspect of their responsibility and submit it back up to the Assistant Secretary who should reach agreement with the Chief Technical Officer. The process is slow and cumbersome and, in an effort to circumvent it, contacts take place at lower levels in the two structures. These very contacts give rise to difficulties. Executive Officers query senior professional officers who resent the level at which the query is raised; often generalist officers do not appreciate the technical problems and the professional officers, intent on getting a job done, do not appreciate the budgetary and political constraints under which the generalist officers must work.

.   .   .

The second problem is one of personnel. There is, first, the question of rewards and prospects, a problem that has a wider range than the public service. In starting pay and in immediate prospects, the professional officer does better than his generalist contemporary unless the latter happens to have entered the service as an Administrative Officer. His ultimate prospects are, however, poorer and his chances of getting to the higher levels of management within the civil service are less. He suffers a disability in that time spent in the university or in temporary employment for the purpose of gaining experience does not normally reckon for superannuation so that he may be unable to attain full pension on retirement. Finally, in experience and training, the professional officer is not given adequate opportunity to develop any inherent administrative talent he may possess. Equally important, though less appreciated, general service staff are not given enough training in the appreciation of problems and methods of a technical nature.[21]

Pointing out that the main aim of its recommendations was to improve the quality of the policy-formulation process and to free the execution of policy from all unnecessary constraints, the group recommended that there should be a unified structure for the performance of each function now organised on a dual structure basis. In practice the group suggested this should be achieved through its particular recommendations on such matters as "grading and remuneration, recruitment and promotion, appraisal, career development and training and retirement and superannuation."[22] These recommendations were (i) that the existing system of classes and grades at the levels covered by their mandate (the higher levels of the civil service) should be abolished; (ii) that all posts should be thrown open to officers possessing the necessary aptitudes, skills and training, and that all barriers of class and departmental location in competition for promotion should be abolished step by step; (iii) that it was absolutely necessary to introduce a rigorous system of staff appraisal and assessment, and to plan a career development programme; (iv) that the existing superannuation provisions be examined with a view to ensuring that they were not a deterrent to late entry into the service, that deferred pension rights be introduced and existing retirement ages reviewed.[23]

Later in the report the group said:

Several essential matters can be attended to at once. First among these, we would put the reform of the present system of promotion. While the full working of a system of promotion by merit will depend on the perfection of the manpower appraisal

---

21.   Op. cit., pars. 10.11.6 and 10.11.8.
22.   ibid., par. 14.7.3.
23.   ibid., pars. 14.7.4–20.

arrangements, the numbers of officers in the higher levels of Departments, i.e. Assistant Principal level and upwards are comparatively small and, in most Departments, the capabilities of officers in these grades are known to the Secretaries and their close advisers. A system of promotion by merit having regard to the needs of each position to be filled should immediately replace all arrangements now existing for promotion by seniority at these levels. Barriers of class and Departmental location should be abandoned in seeking to fill every vacancy with the best man for the job.[24]

The Fulton committee, having analysed the shortcomings of the present structure of the British civil service, also felt that there should be a fundamental change and recommended that classes should be abolished and that all civil servants should be organised in a single grading structure in which there are an appropriate number of different pay levels, matching different levels of skill and responsibility, and in which the correct grading for each post is determined by an analysis of the particular job.[25]

. . . the structure should enable all civil servants, whatever their background, skill or discipline, to make their full contribution to the work of government; in particular, scientific and other specialist staff should be able to bring their professional training and outlook to bear effectively upon today's major problems of policy-making and management. This means an open road to the top of the Service for all kinds of talent. It also means that suitable specialists must be able to take part in policy-making and management at the lower and middle levels of the Service; quite apart from the valuable contributions they can make to management at these levels, it is unrealistic to expect specialists to reach top managerial positions without this earlier experience.[26]

As for the recommendations of the Devlin committee, discussions are going on between the Department of the Public Service and

24. ibid., par. 17.2.2.
25. Op. cit., par. 192.
26. ibid., par. 197.

the two staff associations principally concerned (the Association of Higher Civil Servants and the Institute of Professional Civil Servants) with a view to devising acceptable arrangements. There is a recognition that, for posts in middle and senior management, the aim should be to have all departmental and class barriers removed on a phased basis by service-wide competition in a manner which would have regard to the legitimate aspirations of staff to promotion within their own departments. Matters remaining to be resolved include the number of vacancies within departments to be filled in the normal manner and the number to be filled under any new system; the manner of selection; the examination of the structure in each department to establish what kinds of jobs are required, what responsibilities they entail and the qualities and qualifications of their occupants; the preparation of job specifications which would indicate the essential/desirable attributes required for each post, as well as the experience and qualifications required, together with the determination of appropriate weightings, and the establishment of an acceptable system of staff appraisal and career development.

Conditions of Employment
Traditionally a sense of isolation has surrounded the civil service as an area of employment. To an extent the service has been apart because of the special legal provisions which apply to the recruitment and conditions of employment of civil servants. In recent years the service has become less isolated because of the degree to which questions affecting employment are determined on a national basis. For example, legislation providing for equal pay for men and women was passed in 1974.

In 1975 a bill was circulated, which prohibits discrimination in employment on the basis of sex or marriage. Traditionally certain occupations, such as postman, have been regarded as exclusively male. Similarly, a number of grades such as typist and clerical assistant have traditionally been the preserve of women. The advent of women and men into areas which have been traditionally the preserve of the other sex will no doubt have various social and other effects, at least during the initial period. Also in 1975, arising from the preoccupation of the European Community with employment conditions, the Council of Ministers for Social Affairs agreed on a

draft recommendation in favour of a minimum of four weeks holidays by 31 December 1978. Many civil servants have less than this
number of holidays at present.

At the time of writing, the Employer/Labour Conference, apart
from its participation in the negotiation of national pay agreements,
is also devising a code of fair employment and dismissal procedures.

There are likely to be more developments such as these. Some
of them will apply directly to the civil service and will effect change
in that way. Others will set standards which could well be reflected
in changes in civil service attitudes and procedures.

The Working Environment
Public offices, including those occupied by civil servants, have tended
to be rather drab and dingy. Their sombre décor has had a dispiriting
effect on staff, visitors and potential recruits. The British civil service,
too, has experienced dingy office conditions and the Fulton committee was critical of the effects of these on officials' morale and
efficiency. Appendix 1 of its report said that more needed to be done
to improve physical surroundings:

> The underlying principle that congenial and well-planned con-
> ditions of work can influence efficiency through improved
> morale is one which has gained increasing recognition inside
> and outside the Civil Service in recent years.[27]

In Ireland the subject of improved accommodation has increasingly attracted the attention of both management and staff
sides. On the one hand, the Office of Public Works has succeeded in
accommodating a number of government departments and offices in
new buildings which are a considerable improvement on those which
previously housed them. On the other hand, the staff associations
are reflecting the demands of their members in many other departments in seeking better working conditions.

While the public naturally expect the restraints which apply to
public expenditure generally to be applied with at least an equal
rigour where expenditure on the civil service itself is concerned, it

---

27. *Fulton – The Reshaping of the Civil Service: Developments During 1970,*
(report by the Joint Committee of the National Whitley Council, 1971), p. 29.

can be regarded as one of the responsibilities of management to show an appreciation of the benefits in morale and efficiency that can be produced by an environment which is convenient, attractive and comfortable to work in.

Employment of Married Women

Since the abolition in July 1973 of the requirement that female civil servants should resign on marriage, many women are choosing to combine responsible jobs with looking after their homes and families.

This is also the position in Britain where recently a departmental committee reported on its examination of (i) how far women might be given part-time employment in positions of responsibility, (ii) how it might be made easier for a married woman to combine looking after a family with a civil service career, and (iii) what retraining might be given to make it easier for women to return to civil service employment after a lengthy period of absence. The committee's report, which was accepted in principle by the government, made a number of recommendations, many of which have been implemented already and, where appropriate, have had their scope extended to cover men in similar circumstances.

The report included the following recommendations:

Unpaid leave of up to three years should be available to a woman whose services her Department wishes to retain if she accompanies her husband on a move required by his employment to a place where she cannot continue her own employment in the Civil Service.

Departments should use more widely their discretion in granting both paid and unpaid special leave for urgent domestic affairs. [In Ireland the discretion of departments in this respect is very limited.]

Departments should examine the organisation of their work and consider where appropriate part time work can be provided for serving or former women civil servants . . . who are unable to work full time because they have children to care for. . . .

Where work and staff holiday arrangements permit, Departments should consider sympathetically applications from women who have children at school for some unpaid leave during school holidays. . . .

At least one nursery should be set up for an experimental period
of four years for the children of civil servants . . .; if the experiment proves to be of value to the Civil Service . . . other nurseries
should be set up on a similar basis.[28]

As the years go by, developments similar to those in Britain will,
in all probability, take place in Ireland also.

Conciliation and Arbitration Schemes

As mentioned in chapter 6, the present civil service conciliation and
arbitration scheme came into operation in 1950. Since then, most
other groups in the public service have been covered by similar
schemes so that there are now about ten schemes in force.

Groups covered by these schemes are distinguished by being
excluded by law from access to Labour Court services such as industrial relations officers, rights commissioners and full Labour Court
hearings. It is likely that in the years ahead this exclusion will be
increasingly questioned. Since 1970, public service unions and associations have taken part in national negotiations and have played
an increasingly active role in the affairs of the Irish Congress of
Trade Unions; indeed, a member of a public service union has become president of Congress on more than one occasion. The distinction between public servants and other workers, which was seen in
1946, when the Labour Court was established, as a valid ground for
excluding public servants from the Court, has become increasingly
blurred.

At the request of the Ministers for the Public Service and
Labour, a joint management/Congress working party has been examining the operation of conciliation and arbitration schemes. In an
interim report, it has recommended that, where either side so requests, Labour Court members should serve on arbitration boards.
The working party's next task is a fundamental review of the operation of these schemes, including, in particular, a study of the
possible role of the Labour Court in cases affecting members of the
public service.

Down the years, public service pay has been settled primarily on

---

28. *The Employment of Women in the Civil Service* (London: HMSO, 1971).

the basis of the principle of fair comparison with outside workers. This principle may have to be re-examined critically in the years immediately ahead. The operation of national agreements has tended to clarify pay relationships and to emphasise the ever narrowing circle of comparisons on which pay arguments turn. Many pay settlements in the public service have been criticised on the grounds that the area of comparison has been solely confined to the public service itself. When viewed as a whole, however, the public service is such a large component of total employment that the concept of fair comparison with outside bodies has become increasingly difficult to apply. The conclusion seems irresistible, therefore, that in the years ahead the industrial relations ethos in the public service will become closer to that in the private sector, with consequent questioning of traditional practices and modes of behaviour.

Conclusion
Any changes in the work, organisation and conditions of the civil service deriving from matters to which attention has been drawn in this chapter will no doubt be met with those qualities of resource and dedication which have enabled public servants to adapt to changing times. For, as the Devlin committee noted, the civil service has tried as best it could within the framework of its organisation and resources to promote the development of the nation: ". . . it has given its advice to Ministers fairly and honestly and, when given the final decisions of the Government, it has implemented them without reservation. The civil service has contributed much to what is progressive in our national life."[29]

---

29.   Op. cit., par. 11.2.1.

APPENDIX 1

NET ESTIMATES OF EXPENDITURE AND STAFFING OF
GOVERNMENT DEPARTMENTS

Department	Estimate (£m) (for 1976)	Staff (at January 1975, excluding industrial staff)
Taoiseach	3.0	453
Agriculture and Fisheries ...	122.4	3,759
Defence	85.3	557
Education	268.6	1,025
Finance	68.0	7,581
Foreign Affairs	8.5	616
Gaeltacht	8.1	70
Health	250.0	323
Industry and Commerce ...	86.7	762
Justice	71.9	2,196
Labour	14.9	466
Lands	22.4	1,936
Local Government	93.6	840
Posts and Telegraphs	111.2	22,071
Public Service	11.7	460
Social Welfare	243.2	2,699
Transport and Power	52.5	1,132
Total	**1,522.0**	**46,946**

NUMBER OF CIVIL SERVANTS BY DEPARTMENT AND OFFICE

Department/Office	Staff (at January 1975, excluding industrial staff)
Department of the Taoiseach	46
Central Statistics Office	407
Department of Agriculture and Fisheries ...	3,759
Department of Defence	557
Department of Education	856
National Gallery of Ireland	47
National Library	61
National Museum	61
Department of Finance	328
Chief State Solicitors' Office	73
Houses of the Oireachtas	140
Office of the Attorney General	23
Office of the Comptroller and Auditor General	72
Office of Public Works	824
Office of the Revenue Commissioners	5,448
Ordnance Survey	221
Paymaster General's Office	54
President's Establishment	11
State Laboratory	53
Stationery Office	157
Valuation and Boundary Survey	177
Department of Foreign Affairs	331
Officers serving outside the state	285
Department of the Gaeltacht	70
Department of Health	323
Department of Industry and Commerce	762
Department of Justice	1,223
Circuit Court Offices	247
District Court Clerks Office	103
Land Registry	274
Metropolitan District Courts Offices	96
Public Record Office	26
Registry of Deeds	60
Supreme and High Court Offices	167

Department of Labour	466
Department of Lands and the Land Commission	888
Forest and Wildlife Service	1,048
Department of Local Government	840
Department of Posts and Telegraphs	1,733
Engineering Establishment	6,337
Metropolitan Offices	4,801
Provincial Offices	8,727
Stores Branch	473
Department of the Public Service	286
Civil Service Commission	174
Department of Social Welfare	2,699
Department of Transport and Power	1,132

NUMBER OF CIVIL SERVANTS BY MAJOR GROUPINGS
(January 1975)

Group	Number		
Administrative	1,319	Secretaries and Chairmen of Boards of Commissioners	21
		Deputy Secretaries, Assistant Secretaries and Deputy Assistant Secretaries	141
		Principal	302
		Assistant Principal	709
		Administrative Officer	146
Executive	3,943	Higher Executive Officer	993
		Executive Officer	1,639
		Other Executive Staff (e.g., Inspectors of Taxes, Customs and Excise Officers, Social Welfare Inspectors)	1,311
Clerical	10,817		
Typing	1,440		
Professional, Scientific and Technical (e.g., architects, engineers, legal and medical officers)	3,761		
Inspectorate (e.g., schools inspectors, local government inspectors, driver testers)	1,862		
Supervisory, Minor and Manipulative (e.g., post office clerks, telephonists, postmen, engineering technicians)	21,359		
Messenger	2,445		
Total	**46,946**		

APPENDIX 2

STAFF STRUCTURE OF (I)   GENERAL SERVICE GRADES.
(II) DEPARTMENTAL GRADE OF TAX
INSPECTOR
(III) TYPICAL PROFESSIONAL /
TECHNICAL GRADE

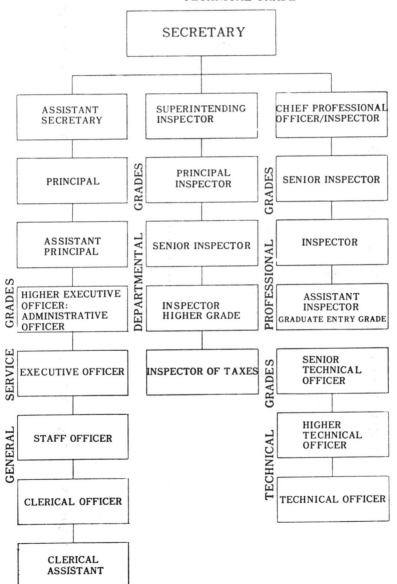

APPENDIX 3

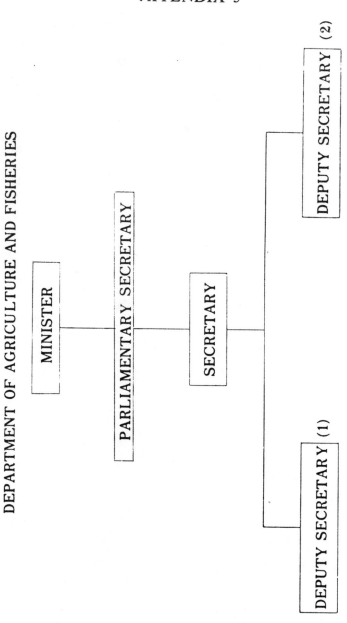

DEPARTMENT OF AGRICULTURE AND FISHERIES

MINISTER

PARLIAMENTARY SECRETARY

SECRETARY

DEPUTY SECRETARY (1)

DEPUTY SECRETARY (2)

NOVEMBER 1975

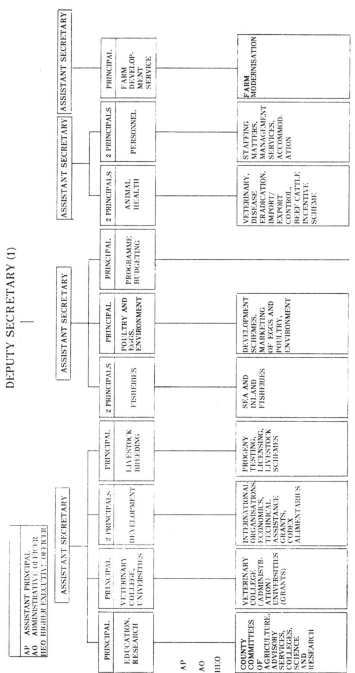

DEPUTY SECRETARY (1)

ASSISTANT SECRETARY | ASSISTANT SECRETARY

AP   ASSISTANT PRINCIPAL
AO   ADMINISTRATIVE OFFICER
HEO HIGHER EXECUTIVE OFFICER

ASSISTANT SECRETARY

PRINCIPAL	2 PRINCIPALS	PRINCIPAL	PRINCIPAL	2 PRINCIPALS
VETERINARY COLLEGE, UNIVERSITIES	DEVELOPMENT	LIVESTOCK BREEDING	FARM DEVELOP-MENT SERVICE	PERSONNEL

PRINCIPAL
EDUCATION, RESEARCH

ASSISTANT SECRETARY

2 PRINCIPALS	PRINCIPAL	PRINCIPAL	2 PRINCIPALS
FISHERIES	POULTRY AND EGGS, ENVIRONMENT	PROGRAMME BUDGETING	ANIMAL HEALTH

AP
AO
HEO

| COUNTY COMMITTEES OF AGRICULTURE, ADVISORY SERVICES, COLLEGES, SCIENCE AND RESEARCH | VETERINARY COLLEGE (ADMINISTR-ATION) UNIVERSITIES (GRANTS) | INTERNATIONAL ORGANISATIONS, ECONOMICS, TECHNICAL ASSISTANCE GRANTS, CODEX ALIMENTARIUS | PROGENY TESTING, LICENSING, LIVESTOCK SCHEMES | SEA AND INLAND FISHERIES | DEVELOPMENT SCHEMES, MARKETING OF EGGS AND POULTRY, ENVIRONMENT | VETERINARY, DISEASE ERADICATION, IMPORT/ EXPORT CONTROL, BEEF CATTLE INCENTIVE SCHEME | STAFFING MATTERS, MANAGEMENT SERVICES, ACCOMMOD-ATION | FARM MODERNISATION |

JUNIOR GRADES: EXECUTIVE OFFICER, STAFF OFFICER, CLERICAL OFFICER, CLERICAL ASSISTANT

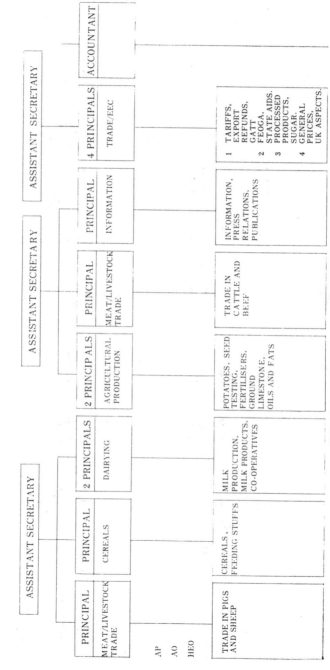

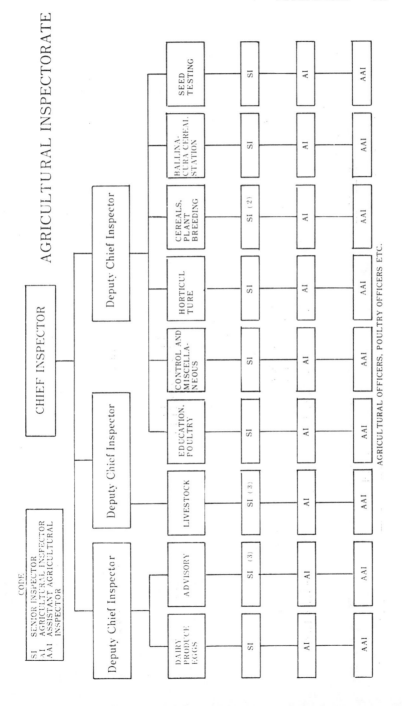

AGRICULTURAL INSPECTORATE

CODE
SI SENIOR INSPECTOR
AI AGRICULTURAL INSPECTOR
AAI ASSISTANT AGRICULTURAL INSPECTOR

CHIEF INSPECTOR

Deputy Chief Inspector | Deputy Chief Inspector | Deputy Chief Inspector

DAIRY PRODUCE, EGGS — SI — AI — AAI

ADVISORY — SI (3) — AI — AAI

LIVESTOCK — SI (3) — AI — AAI

EDUCATION, POULTRY — SI — AI — AAI

CONTROL AND MISCELLANEOUS — SI — AI — AAI

HORTICULTURE — SI — AI — AAI

CEREALS, PLANT BREEDING — SI (2) — AI — AAI

BALLINACURA CEREAL STATION — SI — AI — AAI

SEED TESTING — SI — AI — AAI

AGRICULTURAL OFFICERS, POULTRY OFFICERS ETC.

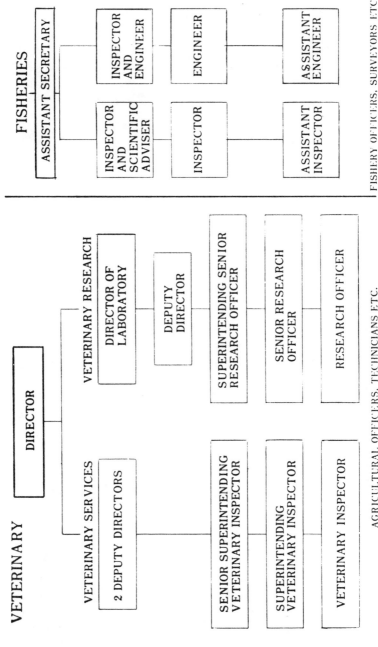

ECONOMIC UNIT

FARM DEVELOPMENT

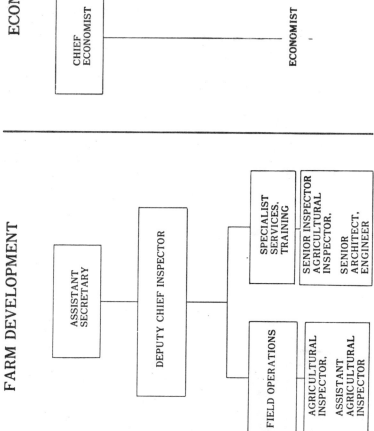

APPENDIX 4

Minutes of Evidence taken before the Committee of Public Accounts

Thursday, 30 November 1972

The Committee met at 11 a.m.

MEMBERS PRESENT:

Deputy Barrett	Deputy MacSharry
„ R. Burke	„ Nolan
„ H. Gibbons	„ Treacy
„ Governey	„ Tunney

Deputy E. Collins in the chair

Mr E. F. Suttle (*Comptroller and Auditor General*) called and examined

VOTE 39—LABOUR

Mr T. Ó Cearbhaill (*Secretary and, therefore, accounting officer, in the Department of Labour*) called and examined

1049. *Chairman.*—Paragraph 69 of the Report of the Comptroller and Auditor General reads:

"*Subhead M.—Grants towards the provision of information and advice for intending emigrants*

This subhead was introduced to enable the Minister for Labour to provide financial assistance to voluntary emigration bureaux within the State and a committee was set up to advise, *inter alia*, on the allocation of grants. The committee recommended token grants only in the year under review."

Mr Suttle.—In the year under review, the Emigrants Advisory Committee recommended only token grants.

1050. *Chairman.*—There is no point in taking this up until the following year's Appropriation Accounts are being examined. We now turn to the Vote itself and firstly to the note on subhead A which refers to the Employment Service. Could the witness expand on this?

Mr Ó Cearbhaill.—This concerns the services operated through the employment exchanges and transferred from the Department of Social Welfare to the Department of Labour. This took place in 1966 and the services continue to be operated by the Department of Labour pending the development of the National Manpower Service when the exchanges will be returned to the Department of Social Welfare, probably in a few months. The policy behind this is to separate the function of job placement from the function of benefit payment. This is in line with policy being developed here and in a number of other countries. A number of placement officers have been recruited and a separate manpower service is being built up.

1051. *Chairman.*—I am very much in favour of a Manpower Service. From an accounting point of view, does the establishment of a Manpower Service mean a duplication with existing services?

Mr Ó Cearbhaill.—No. The employment exchanges are to be returned to the Department of Social Welfare. They will continue to be concerned with the payment of benefits. However, where a particular area might not be covered by the Manpower Service, arrangements would have to be made between the two services whereby these offices might be asked to do certain work for the Manpower Service on an agency basis. The Manpower Service will have definite functions of overseeing the labour situation and the labour market throughout the country at the local level and of trying to match the demand with the supply and *vice versa.*

1052. *Chairman.*—To the extent that the manpower service will be in a separate building from the employment exchange, will this not necessitate extra expenditure?

Mr Ó Cearbhaill.—Yes, but that expenditure will not fall on this Vote. It will be on the Vote for Public Works. There is a very long history here. The employment exchanges, originally called labour exchanges, were set up largely for the purpose of helping workers to get employment, but for various reasons including the addition of benefit-paying functions, the emphasis in their work shifted away from the original purpose. This has been the experience in Britain also. Eventually the policy decision to separate manpower functions from benefit-paying was taken. One of the big practical difficulties was to get employers to use the placement service of the exchanges. Surveys carried out in a number of centres and interviews with employers showed a reluctance to use that service for recruiting workers partly because it was located in buildings where benefit-paying was also carried out.

1053. *Chairman.*—I take it that there will be no duplication of service between employment exchanges and the Manpower Service?

Mr Ó Cearbhaill.—There will be no duplication.

1054. *Deputy MacSharry.*—One is complementary to the other?

Mr Ó Cearbhaill.—That is right. They are separate functions.

1055. *Deputy H. Gibbons.*—I would like to put on record my tribute to the employment service officers in the Sligo area. They are doing very good work in a difficult situation.

Deputy MacSharry.—I second that.

Mr Ó Cearbhaill.—I shall be happy to convey this to the officers concerned.

Chairman.—I do not want to be misinterpreted in what I said. My remarks have been made purely from a manpower point of view.

1056. *Chairman.*—On subhead B.—Travelling and Incidental Expenses—what type of travelling is involved here?

Mr Ó Cearbhaill.—The main elements would be the industrial inspectorate, the Manpower Service and the Labour Court and its Industrial Relations Service.

1057. *Deputy MacSharry.*—On subhead C.—Post Office Services—could you explain the agency fee mentioned in the note?

Mr Ó Cearbhaill.—The Redundancy Payments Scheme is operated on the basis of a stamp for which we negotiate the payment of fees with the Post Office. The Department of Social Welfare had a similar arrangement and there is now a combined stamp covering redundancy and social insurance. The reason for the saving here is that this combined stamp came into operation a short time before the beginning of the year of this account and we had to make a provisional arrangement with them. When the year was over we found we were able to have the actual fee reduced.

1058. *Deputy Treacy.*—On subhead D. Advertising and Publicity—is the exhibition dealing with careers a continuing feature of the work of the Department? Is this beneficial?

Mr Ó Cearbhaill.—Yes. It is not only a continuing but a developing service. There is another subhead which relates to this also but I can answer the Deputy's question here. A number of local groups, such as junior chambers of commerce, past pupils unions, trade unions and others promote career exhibitions. It is an activity in which the Department encourage [sic] them to engage. We supply them with literature, copies of our leaflets and any other information they may want. We take a stand normally at these exhibitions and on occasion we have made small subventions towards the cost. It is a continuing function.

1059. *Deputy Treacy.*—What form does it usually take?

Mr Ó Cearbhaill.—A particular organisation would set about organising an exhibition designed to show young people, mainly school leavers, the type of careers open to them. Many organisations, such as banks, State companies and the Government, say, the Civil Service Commission and the Local Appointments Commission, would be asked to make their information and personnel available to explain to young people the kind of opportunities available to them. The Department would then supply their own leaflets and any other information and would send officers of the Department to man the stand and answer questions.

1060. *Deputy Treacy.*—Are films available for this purpose?

Mr Ó Cearbhaill.—We have been inquiring into this. We have found that films are very costly in a situation like this and also they tend to go out of date and become irrelevant so we have not so far used any films.

1061. *Deputy MacSharry.*—Are the career guidance pamphlets which come from the Department of Labour included in this?

Mr Ó Cearbhaill.—There is a separate subhead—Career Information—for them.

1062. *Deputy H. Gibbons.*—On subhead G—Research—how many manpower surveys have been completed?

Mr Ó Cearbhaill.—When the Department of Labour was set up it was decided as part of this service to experiment with manpower surveys carried out by the Department directly and two areas, Waterford and Galway, were selected for this purpose. These surveys took much longer to carry out than we had hoped and they were also very costly. We then decided we could not continue on this basis so no further surveys of a direct nature have since been carried out. Also, the information which came from these surveys was much too detailed for the requirements of industrial promoters and others. We have now changed over to assisting local groups who wish to do surveys and to organising, in co-operation with the Industrial Development Authority, local surveys of a less intensive nature but which bring forward fairly quickly the manpower information required, especially for a potential industrial promoter interested in an area. I should say, when the National Manpower Service is fully developed, we hope that the type of information coming forward from these special surveys will be available to that Service on a continuing and day to day basis so that we foresee in a few days' time that it may not be necessary, except for some very special reason, to carry out manpower surveys.

1063. *Deputy H. Gibbons.*—Have you any special instructions or standard forms to give to local bodies?

Mr Ó Cearbhaill.—Yes. A number of groups have been assisted by the Department. There is a standard form of questionnaire which is available from the Manpower Service. The Manpower Service are also prepared to advise on how to conduct this and on how to vet the information afterwards.

1064. *Chairman.*—On subhead H— Resettlement Allowances — this re-settlement scheme does not appear to have been very successful in the year under review. Could we have your comment on that?

Mr Ó Cearbhaill.—The scheme was introduced very shortly before the period of this account. Even though it was advertised widely, leaflets were distributed and information on it was circulated through the employment exchanges and through trade union organisations and others, it was not much used. We detected at that time a reluctance by workers to move from one area to another. This scheme was part of the policy of promoting the mobility of workers within the country. We were anxious in a case where an industry might have closed down in a particular area that workers would be helped to move to other areas to get employment. There was at first a strong resistance to this. I should say that since this account we have extended the scope of the resettlement scheme to include the return of emigrant workers to Ireland. These are emigrants with special skills whom we want here. These factors have resulted in quite a big splurge of applications which will be reflected in later accounts.

1065. *Deputy Treacy.*—Have many emigrant workers availed themselves of this service?

Mr Ó Cearbhaill.—Yes. I could not give the number to the Deputy but it is one of the conditions that they will seek employment here through the National Manpower Service. We felt that unless some condition of that kind were introduced the scheme might be abused.

1066. *Chairman.* — Perhaps you would forward a note about the numbers who would benefit under the scheme in general and in particular returning emigrants?

Mr Ó Cearbhaill.—Yes.

1067. *Deputy H. Gibbons.*—I am thinking of a specific case where a person returned in response to an advertisement in the newspapers but he did not get any work. Are you under any obligation in this instance?

Mr Ó Cearbhaill.—Our attitude is that if this scheme were open-ended it might be open to abuse. We would like people to seek employment through the National Manpower Service. If someone comes from England in response to an advertisement but fails to get employment, I think we would be flexible enough to consider the circumstances of the case. However, without knowing the particular case I would not like to comment further.

1068. *Deputy H. Gibbons.*—Some people who return bring their goods and chattels but sometimes they bring too many with them and they are then in trouble with other Departments. Sometimes these goods are regarded as necessary in their business—I am thinking of vans, motor vehicles, machinery and so on. When they take these goods in here they have to pay what they consider excessive duty and in some cases they are not allowed to take them in at all. I am wondering if some thought might be given to this problem?

Chairman.—Perhaps it might be more appropriate to put down a Parliamentary question rather than to discuss it here.

Deputy H. Gibbons.—At any rate, I have thrown out the suggestion and, perhaps, some thought could be given to it.

Mr Ó Cearbhaill.—I understand the Revenue Commissioners have transfer of residence arrangements which might cover some of the remarks of the Deputy.

1069. *Deputy H. Gibbons.*—Would it be possible to convey this in the advertisement or in whatever inducement is given to them to come over so that there will not be any difficulty?

1070. *Chairman.*—I do not think this is the place to deal with it. With regard to subhead I.—Career Information—I should like to compliment the Department on the career guidance leaflets which we get periodically. They are helpful and I hope they are distributed to all the post-primary schools.

Mr Ó Cearbhaill.—Three million leaflets were distributed last year.

1071. *Chairman.*—Is this the first year that has been done?

Mr Ó Cearbhaill.—No, the scheme has been in operation before but it is being developed. The cost of printing is carried by the Stationery Office Vote.

1072. *Deputy MacSharry.*—I had wondered about that because the amount of money appears to have been very small for this necessary work. I should like to compliment the Department on what they have done. Do all Deputies get these leaflets?

Mr Ó Cearbhaill.—I am not sure about that but, if not, it can be arranged.

Chairman.—I agree with the Deputy that Members of both Houses of the Oireachtas should get a copy of these leaflets and, perhaps, this might be arranged.

1073. *Deputy MacSharry.*—In what areas are the leaflets distributed and who gets them?

Mr Ó Cearbhaill.—Anyone who requests a leaflet gets one and thereafter he receives copies on a continuing basis. The leaflets are available in public libraries, in secondary and vocational schools, in emigrants bureaux, in youth clubs, etc. We have an extensive mailing list and anyone who asks for them can get them on a continuing basis if he wishes. However, if the Deputy is aware of any area that has not been included and if he will let the Department know, we will be glad to supply the leaflets.

1074. *Deputy Treacy.*—Are these important leaflets on display and readily available to pupils in the schools? I hope that they are not just filed away.

Mr Ó Cearbhaill.—In the case of schools the Department of Education are developing guidance services. This might be more relevant to the accounting officer of the Department of Education but I know teachers are assigned to this work and are trained for it. They are supplied with copies of these leaflets which they can distribute.

[The examination continued.]

Minutes of the Committee of Public Accounts are published by the Stationery Office and are available from the Government Publications Sale Office or from booksellers.

APPENDIX 5

RECRUITMENT AND SELECTION PROCEDURES (Report of Public Services Organisation Review Group 1966–1969)   TABLE 8.6

Grade	For appointment from outside		For appointment from within	
	Selection Method	Authority	Selection Method	Authority
Executive Officer	Written general knowledge test plus results of leaving certificate examination	Civil Service Commission	Interview Board for eligible Clerical and/or Staff Officers. Written test for eligible Clerical and/or Staff Officers. Departmental selection* for a limited number of staff officers	Department of Finance† Civil Service Commission Individual Department
Higher Executive Officer	Not applicable	—	Departmental selection* from among eligible Executive Officers Interview Board	Individual Department Department of Finance†
Administrative Officer	Written test and personal interview	Civil Service Commission	Written test and personal interview for eligible Executive Officers and corresponding Departmental and professional staff. Departmental and professional staff can normally break in to General Service, only by entry to the AO grade	Civil Service Commission
Assistant Principal	Not applicable	—	Promotion for Administrative Officers after not more than 7 years in grade. Departmental selection* from among eligible Higher Executive Officers	Individual Department Individual Department
Professional Staff	Interview Board, occasionally supplemented by written test	Civil Service Commission	Departmental selection*	Individual Department
Departmental Staff	Normally by written test, occasionally supplemented by Interview Board	Civil Service Commission	Departmental selection*	Individual Department
Clerical Officer	Written test of intermediate certificate standard	Civil Service Commission	Written test and Interview Board (alternate competitions)	Alternately, Department of Finance† and Civil Service Commission
Staff Officer	Not applicable	—	Departmental selection*	Individual Department
Clerk Typist	Typing test (supplemented by shorthand test if applicable); written exam of primary certificate standard for non-typists	Civil Service Commission		

*May or may not involve interview.   †This became the Department of the Public Service in November 1973

APPENDIX 6

CIVIL SERVICE COMMISSION INTERVIEW AND COMPETITION TIMETABLE (Report of Public Services Organisation Review Group 1966–1969)

TABLE 8.7

1. Receipt of request from employing Department to hold competition
2. Preparation of draft regulations
3. Discussion with employing Department (if necessary)
4. Request for sanction of Minister for Finance† to hold the competition
5. Receipt of sanction of Minister for Finance† to hold the competition
6. Taking of certain statutory decisions by Commissioners
7. Despatch of draft regulations to employing Department and to Department of Finance†
8. Receipt of approval of (i) employing Department and (ii) Department of Finance† to draft regulations
9. Receipt of approved conditions of service

Elapsed Time
5 Weeks

10. Advertising of competition
11. Signature of competition regulations by the Commissioners
12. Publication in *Iris Oifigiúil* of statutory notice re making of regulations
13. Issue of application forms to candidates
14. Examination of application forms submitted by candidates
15.* Preparation of Interview Board panel
16. Approval by Commissioners of Interview Board panel
17. Preparation of marking scheme

Elapsed Time
3 Weeks

18. Latest date for receiving completed application forms
19.* Issue of invitations to Board members
20. Arrangement of date of interviews
21. Notify Board members of date of interview
22. Calling of candidates for interview
23. Date of interview
24. Submission to Commissioners of report of Interview Board
25. (i) Approval of Board report by the Commissioners and (ii) formal selection of qualified candidate

Elapsed Time
11 Weeks

26. Issue of provisional recommendation to the employing Department
27. Checking on candidate's character and his claims re qualifications and experiences
28. Receipt of Minister's approval of the candidates provisionally recommended
29. Issue of notices to unsuccessful candidates
30. Medical examination of successful candidate
31. Issue of final recommendation to employing Department (Formal Certificate of Qualification is issued later)

*It is difficult to advance these steps because Board composition depends to an extent on the qualifications needed for applicants which is part of the draft regulations (Steps 2–8).

†This became the Minister/Department of the Public Service in November 1973.

APPENDIX 7

SUMMARY OF SCHEME OF CONCILIATION AND ARBITRATION FOR THE CIVIL SERVICE

General Council

Under the scheme there are two types of council, namely, a general council (for the civil service as a whole) and a departmental council (of which there are several, one for each of the individual departments). Broadly speaking, the general council deals with claims from grades which are common to two or more departments; that is to say, it deals with problems which are not of particular application to one department only. For example, a claim for an increased salary scale for clerical officers, for an increase in the rate of children's allowances, for a variation in the weekly hours of work, or for an alteration in the super-annuation code, would be dealt with at general council.

The council consists of a chairman nominated by the Minister for the Public Service and not more than five other official representatives, together with a principal staff representative and not more than five other staff representatives. The official represen-tatives are almost invariably officers from the Department of the Public Service. To facilitate arrangements on the staff side, a panel of staff represen-tatives is formed under the terms of the scheme. This panel consists of repre-sentatives from the various staff as-sociations or groups of associations, on the basis of one representative for each complete 500 members up to 2,000 and one representative thereafter for each complete 2,000 members. The staff representatives who attend meetings of the council are determined by the panel; they vary from meeting to meeting depending on the subjects for discussion.

Claims normally arise within each individual staff association. The mem-bers meet regularly to discuss their particular interests and, after discus-sion, formulate their claims. These are then transmitted to the panel of staff representatives, known as the staff panel. The meetings of the staff panel then consider all the claims which have thus originated in the various associations. In this way the panel can exercise a degree of coordination, can obtain the views of the various as-sociations and can determine the meas-ure of priority to be accorded to the individual claims. When a claim is approved by the panel, it is transmitted by the panel's secretary to the secretary of the official or management side for inclusion on the agenda of the next meeting of the general council. The staff panel of course elects its own chairman (who thus becomes the prin-cipal staff representative) and other officers from amongst those nominated by the individual associations.

The council has two secretaries, both of whom are civil servants. One is nominated by the management side and the other by the staff panel. Meet-ings must be held not less frequently than once every two months, unless in any such period there is no subject for discussion, in which event, by agree-ment between the management and staff side secretaries, it is recorded that no meeting was required.

It is open to either side to put for-ward items for inclusion in the agenda. In practice, of course, the vast majority of the items are put forward by the staff side. Whether items so put for-ward come within the province of the council is a matter for the chairman to decide. However, before any item is excluded, the scheme provides that the council must be given a chance of expressing its views whether it should be included or excluded. Paragraph 23 of the scheme reads as follows:

The subjects appropriate for discussion by the General Council will be:
(a) Principles governing recruitment to general service classes and to professional, scientific and technical classes common to two or more Departments;
(b) Claims for increase or decrease of pay of the Civil Service as a whole;
(c) Claims relating to general service classes and to professional, scientific and technical classes common to two or more Departments in relation to (i) pay and allowances whether in the nature of pay or otherwise, (ii) overtime rates, (iii) subsistence allowances, (iv) travelling, lodging and disturbance allowances, (v) removal expenses;
(d) Principles governing remuneration and form of payment of additional remuneration, viz., whether by way of continuing allowance or periodic gratuity;
(e) Hours of weekly attendance of general service classes;
(f) Principles of promotion in the general service classes and in professional, scientific and technical classes which are common to two or more Departments;
(g) Principles governing discipline;
(h) Suggestions by the staff of general application for promoting efficiency in the Civil Service;
(i) General considerations in regard to the grading of general service classes and of professional, scientific and technical classes common to two or more Departments;

(j) Principles governing superannuation;
(k) Principles governing the grant of annual, sick and special leave;
(l) Claims relating to establishment of a proportion of unestablished general service and professional, scientific and technical classes common to two or more Departments;
(m) Questions of doubt or difficulty in relation to the subjects appropriate for discussion at Departmental Councils.

It appears an unusual arrangement that the chairman of the council should, in effect, be a member of the management side. It applies also in the case of the departmental councils, which will be described later, where the chairman is either the head of the department or the assistant secretary with responsibilities in the personnel area. Such an arrangement is not usual in other areas of dispute. It appears to give satisfaction to both sides, however, since when the scheme was revised in 1973 no change was made in the long standing practice. In addition to the foregoing items, the staff side may bring forward for discussion such other items as the Minister for the Public Service may consider appropriate from time to time.

Council Reports

It is not within the competence of the council to make agreements binding on the Minister for the Public Service but the council may make agreed recommendations or may, at the request of either side, record disagreement. Reports of all discussions which take place at meetings of the general council are signed by the secretaries of the council and are then deemed to be agreed reports. Agreed reports are submitted to the Minister for the Public Service and also to the staff side of the council. Decisions of the Minister for the Public Service on matters discussed at the general council are conveyed to the staff side secretary of the council. (What this means in practice is that no offers are made by the management side unless it knows that the offer will in fact have the approval of the Minister for the Public Service.) The council has power to set up sub-committees to examine particular matters and these are, indeed, a feature of its operations. The proceedings of the council are confidential and no statements concerning them are issued except with its authority.

Departmental Councils

Each department has its own departmental council to deal with matters relating particularly to its own staff. Claims for pay which are put forward by departmental grades, e.g., building inspectors, agricultural officers or foresters, are heard at the councils in the Departments of Local Government, Agriculture and Fisheries and Lands respectively. Such councils also hear claims for the redress of local grievances on behalf of general service grades, that is, the councils deal, for example, with claims for improved accommodation or for the provision of local welfare services.

Each council consists of a chairman and not more than three other official representatives, together with a principal staff representative and not more than three other staff representatives. Each department has its own staff panel which is composed of representatives of the staff associations for the various categories of staff employed in the Department. The size of the staff panel and its membership is a matter for arrangement between the associations themselves or, failing agreement, by the panel of staff representatives attached to the general

council. Paragraph 36 of the scheme prescribes as follows:

The staff representatives must be (a) civil servants serving in the Department who are members of the classes represented by associations recognised for the purpose of staff representation in the Department, or (b) whole-time officials of such associations, or (c) subject, on the occasion of each attendance, to the consent of the Head of the officer's Department where it is proposed to take special leave, part-time officials of such associations serving in other Departments.

As in the case of general council, the departmental council has two secretaries, each an officer of the department — one nominated by the management side and the other by the staff side. The procedure for, and frequency of, meetings is similar to that described in the case of general council. The subjects for discussion are also broadly similar to those appropriate to the general council. As in the case of the general council, it is not within the competence of departmental councils to make binding agreements but the council may make agreed recommendations or may, at the request of either side, record disagreement. What this provision means in practice is that no offer may be made by the official side without the prior approval of the Department of the Public Service.

The necessity for having the prior approval of the Department of the Public Service derives from that Department's responsibilities in relation to all aspects of pay and conditions. It would serve no useful purpose to have an agreed recommendation rejected by the Minister for the Public Service because his Department did not agree with the terms of the settlement. It is sometimes held that this necessary arrangement places the parties engaged in discussion at departmental council level in an unreal situation. On the one hand the staff side know that in the last analysis the real decision-makers are not those sitting across the table from them, although, of course, these persons must be convinced in the first place. On the other hand the management side occasionally find their hands tied by the Department of the Public Service when they themselves wish to make an offer on, or to concede, a claim. Again, as in the case of the designation of chairman of the council, the fact that the arrangement appears to work to the general satisfaction of all concerned, seems to indicate that in practice it does not lead to any dissatisfaction.

Arbitration

Where claims made by the staff side, either at the general council or at the various departmental councils, are disagreed, i.e. where the management side is unable to make an offer acceptable to the staff side, the latter may then elect, if the claim is an arbitrable one, to ask to have it brought to arbitration. Broadly speaking, arbitrable claims are those for, or in regard to, the rates or the amount of (i) pay and allowances in the nature of pay, (ii) overtime, (iii) total weekly hours of work, (iv) annual and sick leave, (v) subsistence allowances, (vi) travelling, lodging and disturbance allowances.

The arbitration board consists of a chairman and four other members, two of whom are civil servants nominated by the Minister for the Public Service and two are civil servants or whole-time officials nominated by the staff panel of the general council. The chairman is appointed by the government on the nomination of the Minister for the Public Service in agreement with the staff side. Members of the

Oireachtas, serving civil servants or members of staff associations are ineligible for appointment as chairman.

Certain procedures are laid down for dealing with cases at arbitration. Where arbitration is sought by a staff association, the association must send a statement of its case together with terms of reference to the secretary of the Department of the Public Service. This statement, together with a counter statement prepared by the management side, is then sent to the secretary of the arbitration board. The counter statement is also sent to the staff association which is making the claim.

The chairman of the board submits to the Minister for the Public Service a report on every claim submitted to the board. This report is signed by the chairman only and no other report is issued. It indicates whether the report is unanimous, is a majority report or is the finding of the chairman himself. The Minister for the Public Service must then, within a period of one month, present the report to Dáil Eireann. The report is not published before such presentation.

The scheme distinguishes between two different kinds of report. In the case of a report which does not concern a claim for the general revision of civil service pay, the Minister for the Public Service must, subject to what follows, authorise the implementation of the report within one month of his receiving it. If, however, the minister feels that the board's findings should not be accepted or should for any reason be brought to the notice of the government, he submits the report to the government. The government then either authorises the implementation of the finding within three months of the time it was received by the minister or introduces a motion in the Dáil recommending either the rejection of the finding or such other recommendation as it sees fit.

Paragraph 72 of the scheme provides that if a report of the board concerns a claim for a general revision of civil service pay, the government must adopt one of the following courses:

(1) (a) [within three months of the date of the receipt of the report by the Minister for the Public Service] signify that they propose to give immediate effect to the finding of the Board in full;

(b) as soon as may be after the expiration of the three months after the date of the receipt of the report by the Minister for the Public Service introduce a motion in Dáil Eireann (i) proposing the rejection of the finding, or (ii) proposing the modification of the finding, or (iii) proposing (because they consider that it would not be possible, without imposing additional taxation, to give full effect to the finding within the current financial year) the deferment of a final decision on the report until the Budget for the next following financial year is being framed and indicating to what extent, if any, they propose in the interval, without prejudice to the final decision, to give effect to the finding, the extent of the payment in that event to be determined by the amount which can be met without imposing additional taxation.

(2) Should Dáil Eireann have approved of a motion presented to it in accordance with the terms of sub-paragraph (1) (b) (iii) preceding, the Government will, save in entirely exceptional circumstances, make full provision in the Budget for the following financial year for the annual charge appropriate to that financial year in respect of the report of the arbitration board and also for the amount necessary, as an addition to any amount already paid, to give full effect to the board's finding from the date of operation recommended in the report to the end of the financial year in which the report was presented to Dáil Eireann. Where the Government do not so propose to give effect to the board's finding, they will introduce a motion in Dáil Eireann indicating the action they propose to take and recommending such action to the House.

APPENDIX 8

CIVIL SERVANTS AND POLITICS

Statement at a press conference at Leinster House, 6 March 1974 by the Minister for the Public Service, Mr Richie Ryan, TD.

The government has decided that:

1. State industrial employees and civil servants in manipulative sub-clerical and manual grades will be free to engage in political activity unconditionally.

2. Civil servants of the clerical classes and of non-manipulative and sub-professional classes in similar salary ranges will in future be eligible for freedom to engage in political activity subject only to a proviso that the Minister for the Public Service on the recommendation of the minister in charge of a particular department might declare that such freedom should not apply to officers engaged in a particular category of work.

3. Officers in the Department of Posts and Telegraphs who do not come within the ambit of the two previously enumerated groups and who at present enjoy limited political freedom will continue to enjoy such rights unchanged.

4. In no case, either in the civil service or in the industrial area, will freedom of political activity extend to standing for election to either House of the Oireachtas.

5. Civil servants involved in the framing of policy proposals will remain completely barred from political activities, this embargo to embrace administrative and middle management grades in the general service.

The government will review the position generally after a period of three years.

The government considers that in a democratic society it is desirable that as many citizens as possible should play an active part in the public affairs of the community.

At the same time the government is convinced that the public interest demands that confidence be maintained in the political impartiality of civil servants.

The government is satisfied that the high standards of integrity and impartiality which are a proud feature of the Irish civil service will continue to be observed in the future. While the right to take part in political activities is one which everybody, including public servants, should be as free as possible to exercise, the government considers that the public interest requires that it be limited in some cases.

For instance, the public interest would appear to require that civil servants concerned with the framing of policy proposals should serve, and be seen to serve, all governments objectively and impartially. It is also desirable that civil servants whose work concerns the execution of policy and entails, for instance, a direct service to the public in confidential areas should not be known adherents of a particular party or be known to have personal political ambitions. The government therefore considers that at this time it would be inappropriate to confer full political freedom on civil servants in the senior and administrative and middle management grades. On the other hand it would be unfair to withhold political freedom from employees in the manipulative, sub-clerical and manual grades who are not engaged in work of a political character. As sub-postmasters are not employees but contractors, it is considered that they too should be free, if they so wish, to engage in political activity.

The government has taken these steps in the conviction that they are fully justified having regard to the political maturity of our society, the established integrity of the public service and the desirability of encouraging the fullest use of civil rights consistent with the public interest.

Civil Service Publications

The Stationery Office is the body responsible for all official publications. It publishes an annual catalogue of government publications which is available free on request. The publications may be purchased from the Government Publications Sale Office, GPO Arcade, Dublin 1 or from booksellers. Regular publications on the civil service and its activities include:

(i) annual reports of ministers on the work of their departments,

(ii) estimates of expenditure for public services for each financial year,

(iii) an annual *Directory of State Services* which includes particulars of the staffing, including numbers, in each department and office, as well as civil service pay and allowances,

(iv) examination papers for the various entrance examinations to the civil service.

A considerable amount of information about the civil service, including the work and staffing of the departments, is contained in the *Administration Yearbook and Diary* published annually by the Institute of Public Administration.

Many of the departments and offices issue pamphlets and leaflets about aspects of the work for which they are responsible; for example, the Civil Service Commission provides material on career opportunities in the civil service, the Department of Agriculture and Fisheries on various aspects of farming activities and the Department of Social Welfare on benefits available to social welfare recipients.

Bibliography

1. Books and Pamphlets

Chubb, Basil	*The Government and Politics of Ireland.* London: Oxford University Press, 1970. Chapter 9. "The Central Administration and the Civil Service".
	A Source Book of Irish Government. Dublin: Institute of Public Administration, 1964.
Chubb, Basil and Thornley, David	*Irish Government Observed.* Dublin: reprinted from *The Irish Times,* 1965.
Cohan, Al	*The Irish Political Elite.* Dublin: Gill and Macmillan, 1972.
Delany, V. T. H.	*The Administration of Justice in Ireland.* 4th edition by Charles Lysaght. Dublin: Institute of Public Administration, 1975.
Finlay, Ian	*The Civil Service.* Dublin: Institute of Public Administration, 1966.
Grogan, Vincent	*Administrative Tribunals in the Public Service.* Dublin: Institute of Public Administration, 1961.
Hensey, Brendan	*The Health Services of Ireland.* 2nd revised edition. Dublin: Institute of Public Administration, 1972.
Hoctor, Daniel	*The Department's Story: A History of the Department of Agriculture.* Dublin: Institute of Public Administration, 1971.
I.O. (C.J.C. Street)	*The Administration of Ireland, 1920.* London: Philip Allan, 1921.
Lemass, S. F.	"The Organization behind the Economic Programme", in Basil Chubb and Patrick Lynch (eds.), *Economic Development and Planning.* Dublin: Institute of Public Administration, 1969.

Leon, D. E.   *Advisory Bodies in Irish Government*. Dublin: Institute of Public Administration, 1963.

Lynch, Patrick   "Change and the Public Service", in Basil Chubb and Patrick Lynch (eds.), *Economic Development and Planning*. Dublin: Institute of Public Administration, 1969. Also in *Irish Banking Review*, June 1967, 17–24.

McDowell, R. B.   *The Irish Administration, 1801–1914*. London: Routledge and Kegan Paul, 1964.

Meghen, P. J.   *A Short History of the Public Service*. Dublin: Institute of Public Administration, 1962.

O'Connell, J. B.   *Financial Administration of Saorstát Eireann, with an epitome of the reports of the Committee on Public Accounts 1922–32*. Dublin: Browne and Nolan, 1934. Revised edition. *Financial Administration of Ireland*. Dublin: Mount Salus Press, 1960.

O'Donnell, James D.   *How Ireland is Governed*. 5th edition. Dublin: Institute of Public Administration, 1975.

O Muimhneacháin, M.   *The Functions of the Department of the Taoiseach*. Dublin: Institute of Public Administration, 1960. Also in *Administration*, VII, 4 (1959), 277–93.

Pyne, Peter   *The Irish Bureaucracy: its political role and the environmental factors influencing this role: Some preliminary remarks*. Londonderry: New University of Ulster, Institute of Continuing Education. (Occasional Paper No. 1 1973). Bibliographical notes. [Revised version of a paper read to the Comparative Administration Workshop of the European Consortium for Political Research at the University of Mannheim, April 1973].

Raven, J. and
Whelan, C. T.

Pilot Material from General Survey of Attitudes and Values in Ireland. [Unpublished paper read at Irish-Norwegian Seminar on Political Behaviour and Attitudes. Dublin: Economic and Social Research Institute, 1972].

Committee on Post-Entry Education of Public Servants: Report. Dublin: Institute of Public Administration, 1959.

The Constructive Work of Dáil Eireann. (A series of pamphlets on the National Police and Courts of Justice, the Department of Agriculture and the Land Settlement Commission, the Commission of Enquiry into the Resources and Industries of Ireland and the Department of Trade and Commerce) Dublin: Talbot Press, 1921.

The Department of Industry and Commerce. Dublin: Institute of Public Administration, 1961. Also in *Administration*, IX, 2 (1961), 120–47.

Department of Transport and Power. Dublin: Institute of Public Administration, 1965. Also in *Administration*, XIII, 4 (1965), 296–315.

Mobility in the Public Service: Report of Committee. Dublin: Institute of Public Administration, 1961. Chairman: C. S. Andrews.

Organizing for Maximum Efficiency in the Public Service, discussion paper 1. Dublin: Institute of Public Administration, 1959.

Report of Public Services Organisation Review Group 1966–1969: Summary [Devlin Report]. Dublin: Institute of Public Administration, 1970.

2. Periodicals

Baker, T. J.   [Research and the Devlin Report]. *Public Affairs*, II, 5 (January 1970), 9–10.

Barrington, T. J.   "Cupidi Rerum Novarum". *Administration,* VIII, 1 (1960), 19–35.
"Machinery of Government". *Administration*, XI, 3 (1963), 187–206.
"The Next Necessary Thing". *Administration*, VII, 2 (1959), 118–41. "Discussion: 'The Next Necessary Thing'—in the civil service". *Administration*, VIII, 1 (1960), 72-82. [Reprint of discussion in *Civil Service Review* following publication of article by T. J. Barrington.]
"Selection in the Civil Service". *Administration*, IV, 3 (1956), 56–79.
"Some Aspects of Recruitment Examinations for the Public Service". *Administration*, XI, 2 (1963), 152–62.

Boland, F. H.   "Diplomatic Devlin . . ." *Public Affairs*, II, 7 (March 1970), 4–7. [Devlin on the Department of External Affairs.]

Breathnach, Breandán "An Roinn Talmhaiochta agus an Ghaeltacht". *Administration*, II, 2 (1954), 48–52.

Ceannt, E. T.   "Training". *Administration*, III, 2–3 (1955), 34–48.

Christopher, Ralph   "Promotion Policy". *Administration*, XXI, 3 (1973), 345–54.

Chubb, Basil   "Do Public Servants in Ireland Need an Institute?" *Administration*, II, 2 (1954), 13–26.

Civil Service Training Centre   Civil Service Training Centre Report of Activities 1964–65. *O & M Record* (Department of Finance), No. 8 (Lunasa 1965), 142–70.
Second Annual Report in *O & M Record*, No. 14 (Lunasa 1966), 254–86.

Annual Report of the Civil Service Training Centre for the year ended 31 July 1967. *O & M Record*, No. 19 (February 1968), 344–77.

Condon, D.   "The Bureaucrat Observed. III: Executive Thinking—A Survey". *Administration*, II, 1 (1954), 75–86.

Curran, R. J.   "The Machinery of Government: Some Observations". *Administration*, XII, 2 (1964), 102–10.

de Fréine, S.   "Delegation of Authority in Civil Service Departments: A Comparative Study based on the Grant of Signing Powers". *O & M Record* (Department of Finance), 22 (Bealtaine 1968), 407–21.

de Paor, Neans   "Women in the Civil Service". *Administration*, III, 2–3 (1955), 141–47.

Deeny, James   "The Bureaucrat Observed. II: The Professional Civil Servant". *Administration*, I, 3 (1953), 57–63.

Department of Finance   "Staff Development in the Civil Service: Preliminary Memorandum". *Dul Chun Cinn*, 13 (April 1972), 225–65.

Devlin, Liam St J.   "Report of the Public Services Organisation Review Group: The Finance Function in the Public Service". *Administration*, XVIII, 4 (1970), 302–13.

Dooney, Seán   "Looking at the Civil Service". *Administration*, XX, 3 (1972), 59–86 (81–85 deal with Ireland).
"Programmed Instruction and its Use in Civil Service Training". *Administration*, XIII, 3 (1965), 226–38.

Doyle, T.   "Public Service: Civil Service Recruitment". *Public Affairs*, IV, 8 (April 1972), 6–7.

Dunne, Jim   "Of Ombudsmen and Aireachts". *Business and Finance*, X, 17 (17 January 1974), 14.

Fairbanks, J.
"The Income of the Higher Civil Servant". *Administration*, III, 2–3 (1955), 59–68.

Finlay, Ian
"La Fonction Publique Irlandaise". [The Irish Civil Service]. *International Review of Administrative Sciences (Brussels)*, XXXIV, 1 (1968), 25–31. Summary in English.

FitzGerald, Garret
"Training Public Servants for National Development". *Administration*, VII, 4 (1959–60), 337–48.

Gaffey, Peter
"The Organisation Function in the Public Service". *Administration*, XIX, 1 (1971), 22–32.
"Programme Budgeting and the Organisation and Personnel Function". *Administration*, XVIII, 4 (1970), 314–25.

Gaffney, Séamus
"Adiestramiento para la Función Pública Irlandesa". [The Training of Civil Servants] *International Review of Administrative Sciences* (Brussels), XXXIV, 1 (1968), 32–38. Summary in English.
"Increasing the Efficiency of the Civil Service". *Irish Banking Review*, March 1967, 18–27.
"Irish Civil Servants in Training". *Administration*, XIII, 1 (1965), 39–47.
"Recruitment to the Irish Civil Service". *Irish Banking Review,* March 1969, 19–31. Reprinted in *Administration*, XVIII, 2 (1970), 159–73.
"Towards Greater Efficiency". *Administration,* XIII, 2 (1965), 98–106.

Harbison, J. H.
"The Devlin Report". *Management*, XVI, 10 (October 1969), 7–10. [Review of Report of Public Services Organisation Review Group].

Hart, Ian
"Education and the Public Service". *Léargas*, 9 (January-February 1967), 6–9. Part 2. *Léargas*, 10 (June-July 1967), 7–11.

"Executive Morale in the Civil Service".
Administration, XVII, 2 (1969), 59–64.
"Executive Officers in the Civil Service:
Survey of Post-Secondary Education. Part
1". *Administration*, XVI, 3 (1968), 255–80.
Part 2, *Administration*, XVII, 1 (1969),
59–63.
"Public Opinion on Civil Servants and the
Role and Power of the Individual in the
Local Community". *Administration*, XVIII,
4 (1970), 375–91.

Kelly, Desmond   "Planning Ahead in Irish Civil Service
Training". *Public Affairs*, II, 1 (September
1969), 17–19.

Leon, Donald E.   "Inter-Departmental Committees and the
Advisory Process". *Administration*, X, 4
(1962), 381–93.

Linehan, Thomas P.   "The Bureaucrat Observed. IV: The Growth
of the Civil Service". *Administration*, II, 2
(1954), 61–73.

Lynch, Patrick   "Administrative Theory and the Civil Service". *Administration*, IV, 4 (1956–57),
97–116.

MacCormac, M. J.   "The Devlin Report: A Review". *Administration*, XVII, 3 (1969), 309–18.

Meghen, P. J.   "Estimates and Estimates Speeches. No. 3:
The Department of Health". *Léargas*, 5
(February–March 1966), 9–11.
"Estimates and Estimates Speeches. No. 4:
The Department of Industry and Com-
merce". *Léargas*, 6 (April–May 1966), 7–9.
"Estimates and Estimates Speeches: The
Department of Justice". *Léargas*, 4 (Oc-
tober–November 1965), 9–11.
"Estimates and Estimates Speeches: The
Department of Transport and Power".
Léargas, 5 (December 1965–January 1966),
9–10.

"Making a New Department". [Department of Labour]. *Léargas*, 7 (June–July 1966), 1–7.

Murphy, Christina — "Women in the Public Service". *Public Affairs*, VI, 1 (September 1973), 2–3.

Murphy, John — "Yet More Devlin — Agriculture and Lands". *Public Affairs*, II, 4 (December 1969), 7–8. [Followed by personal policy and inside opinion, 8–10. (reprinted from *Civil Service Review*, October 1969)].

[Murray, Seán] — "Reviewing the Civil Service". *Léargas*, 6 (April–May 1966), 1–6.

Nagle, J. C. — "Agricultural Administration". *Administration*, II, 2 (1954), 39–47.

O Cearbhaill, Tadhg — "The Department of Labour and the Future". *Administration*, XV, 2 (1967), 138–43.
"The Role of the Department of Labour". *Administration*, XV, 1 (1967), 1–5.

O'Conaill, S. — "Towards Greater Efficiency in the Irish Civil Service". *International Review of Administrative Sciences (Brussels)*, XXXIV, 1 (1968), 21–24.

O'Connor, T. P. — *The Higher Civil Service in Ireland: Its Role, Recruitment and Training.* Dublin University, unpublished M Litt Thesis, 1967.
"Higher Civil Service Training. 2. Setting the Scene for On the Job Training". *Public Affairs*, I, 1 (October 1968), 16–17.
"Higher Civil Service Training. 3. Induction: the Environmental Framework". *Public Affairs*, I, 3 (December 1968), 14–16.

O'Connor, T. P. and Wilding, R. W. L. — "The Civil Service in the Modern State". *Studies,* LIX, 234 (1970), 164–79.

O Mahony, Seán — "Programme Budgeting in the Department of Education". *Administration*, XIX, 3 (1971), 222–31.

"The Working of the First Programme Budget in Education". *Administration*, XX, 3 (1972), 16–26.

O Mathúna, Seán   "The Christian Brothers and the Civil Service". *Administration*, III, 2–3 (1955), 69–74.

"Diaspora". *Administration*, I, 2 (1953), 62–68. [Government departments — decentralisation].

O Muireadhaigh, T.   "The Bureaucrat Observed. 1. A Personal View". *Administration*, I, 1 (1953), 51–58.

O Raifeartaigh, T.   "The State's Administration of Education". *Administration*, II, 4 (1954–55), 67–77.

Ó Slatarra, P.   "Authority and the Public Servant". *Administration*, VI, 3 (1958), 240–46.

Pyne, Peter   "The Bureaucracy in the Irish Republic: Its Political Role and the Factors Influencing It". *Political Studies*, XXII, 1 (1974), 15–30. [Revised version of paper to Comparative Administration Workshop of European Consortium for Political Research at the University of Mannheim, April 1973].

"The Irish Civil Service". *Administration*, XXII, 1 (1974), 26–59. [Revised version of paper to Comparative Administration Workshop of European Consortium for Political Research at University of Mannheim, April 1973].

Roche, D.   "The Civil Servant and Public Relations". *Administration*, XI, 2 (1963), 104–08.

"School of Public Administration". *Administration*, XII, 3 (1964), 230–38.

Scott, Dermot   "The Bureaucrat at Bay". *Léargas*, 11 (November 1967) [Civil service reform: an analysis of the present discussion].

Smyth, William   "The Location of the Personnel Management Function". *Administration*, XIII, 4 (1965), 324–58. (Section IV "Ireland", 338).

"The Responsibility of the Civil Servant in Ireland". *Administration*, XXIII, 4 (1975), 339–61.

Smyth, William (Editor)

"The Devlin Report". *Administration*, XVII, 3 (1969), 225–30.

Waldron, J. J.

"The Irish Customs and Excise". *Administration*, V, 4 (1957), 35–53.

Whelan, Noel

"The Irish Public Service. Aspects of Future Progress". *Business and Finance*, X, 14 (20 December 1973), 33.

"Organisation and Management in the Public Sector". *Administration*, XXI, 4 (1973), 396–404.

"Public Service Department: The Organisation Function". *Public Affairs*, IV, 10 (June 1972), 3 and 5.

Whitaker, T. K.

"The Administrator and the Professional in the Irish Public Service". *Léargas*, February-March 1966, 4–7.

"The Finance Attitude". *Administration*, II, 3 (1954), 61–68. Reprinted in B. Chubb and P. Lynch (eds.), *Economic Development and Planning*. Dublin: Institute of Public Administration, 1969. Chapter III.

"The Civil Service and Development". *Administration*, IX, 2 (1961), 83–87.

Wright, Maurice

"The Responsibility of the Civil Servant in Great Britain". *Administration*, XXIII, 4 (1975), 362–95.

3. Miscellaneous

Administration Yearbook and Diary. Dublin: Institute of Public Administration. Annual. 1967–

"Attitudes and Morale of Civil Servants in Ireland and the UK". *Public Affairs*, I, 5 (February 1969), 7. [Note on survey of executive officers by Ian Hart, later published in *Administration*, XVII, 1 (1969), 59–64.]

"Department of the Public Service: Fourth Aireacht Announced". *Public Affairs*, V, 5 (January 1973), 5. [Department of Local Government].

"Department of the Public Service: An Overview". *Public Affairs*, V, 3 (December 1972), 3–4.

"Department of the Public Service: The Personnel Function". *Public Affairs*, V, 3 (December 1972), 2–3.

"Department of the Public Service: Remuneration". *Public Affairs*, V, 3 (November 1972), 4–5.

"Department of the Public Service: The Organisation Division". *Public Affairs*, V, 3 (November 1972), 2–4.

"Departments of State à la Devlin". *Public Affairs*, II, 3 (November 1969), 12–13.

[Devlin Report] *Administration*, XVII, 4 (1969), 339–436. [Special issue on Devlin Report. Contributors: R. C. O'Connor, L. St J. Devlin, T. J. Barrington, P. Gaffey, Sir G. Thompson, Sir W. Armstrong, Harold Seidman, R. J. Lawrence, N. Johnson].

"Devlin: the Public Service Department". *Public Affairs*, IV, 1 (1971), 8–9.

"Devlin Report: the CII's view". *Public Affairs*, II, 9 (May 1970), 11–12.

"Devlin Report: the basic concepts". *Public Affairs*, II, 2 (October 1969), 6–8 and 19–20.

"Dr Whitaker Retires: interview". *Public Affairs*, I, 6 (March 1969), 4–6.

The Educational Needs of the Higher Public Service. Report of Working Party set up by the Institute of Public Administration.

Chairman: J. A. Scannell. *Local and Public Forum*, III, 3 (Autumn 1972), 9, 11, 13, 15, 17–18. Also in *Administration*, XX, 3 (1972), 41–58.

"Efficiency in the Civil Service: A Symposium". *Administration*, I, 1 (1953), 7–36. [Contributors: L. M. FitzGerald, J. A. Scannell, S. O Conaill, H. J. Mundow, E. Ceannt, D. Herlihy, J. Collins, T. J. Barrington].

"Employer-Labour Conference on Higher Public Service Pay". *Local and Public Forum*, III, 4 (1972), 17–21. [The Conference's examination of the Report of the Review Body on Higher Remuneration. . . .]

"Government and Communications". [Summary Address by An Taoiseach Mr Jack Lynch, 9 November 1970, on the need for a flow of information from the civil service to the general public] *Public Affairs*, III, 3 (November 1970), 2–3.

"The Idea of a Profession". [Paper added to research report on School of Public Administration, January 1971] *Administration*, XIX, 1 (1971), 50–60.

"Organisation and Management in the Public Sector". [summary of] an address to the Institution of Engineers of Ireland in November 1973 by Dr Noel Whelan, *Public Affairs*, VI, 4 (December 1973), 6.

"Post-Entry Education for Civil Servants: Report of Joint Management-Staff Working Party". *Administration*, XX, 3 (1972), 27–40. [Working party set up by Department of Finance. Chairman: Sean Ó Conchobhair].

"The Public Servant, the Citizen and the Law". *Léargas*, 6 (February–March 1966), 1–4. [Mr. Justice Kenny. Decision in case

MacAuley v. *Minister for Posts and Telegraphs*].
"School of Public Administration: Evaluation". *Administration*, XIX, 1 (1971), 33–49.
"Son of Devlin". *Public Affairs*, V, 2 (October 1972), 1. [Review Body on Higher Remuneration in the Public Sector].
"Structure of the Civil Service". 1. 'Some Facts' by M. D. McCarthy. 2. 'Elaborate Contrivance' by T. J. Barrington. *Administration*, III, 2–3 (1955), 75–108.

4. Official Publications

Commission of Inquiry into the Civil Service 1932–35. Reports and evidence. 3 vols. Dublin; GPSO, 1935.

Department of
Finance

The Civil Service. Dublin: Department of Finance, 1965.
Report of the Tribunal of Inquiry into the Rates of Remuneration Payable to Clerical Recruitment Grades in the Public Sector of the Economy. Chairman: G. Quinn. Dublin: Stationery Office, 1966.

Department of the
Public Service

Restructuring the Department of Health: The Separation of Policy and Execution. Dublin: Stationery Office, 1973.
Restructuring the Department of Transport and Power: The Separation of Policy and Execution. Dublin: Stationery Office, 1974.
Committee on Public Accounts Reports. Dublin: Stationery Office, 1922–23.

Directory of State Services. Dublin: Stationery Office, Annual. 1966–
Estimates for Public Services. Annual. 1922–23—

Report of Public Services Organisation Review Group 1966–1969. Presented to the Minister for Finance. Dublin: Stationery Office, 1969. Chairman: Liam St John Devlin.

Review Body on Higher Remuneration in the Public Sector. Report to the Minister for Finance on:

(1) General levels of remuneration appropriate to civil servants, local authority and health board officers outside the scope of conciliation and arbitration schemes and chief executives of state-sponsored bodies.

(2) The levels of remuneration of members of the Government, Parliamentary Secretaries, Attorney General and Chairman and Deputy Chairman of Dáil Eireann and Seanad Eireann and allowances of members of the Houses of the Oireachtas.

(3) The levels of remuneration of the judiciary. Dublin: Stationery Office, 1972. Chairman: Liam St John Devlin.

Addenda

Chapman, Ralph J. K.   "The Irish Public Service: Change or Reform". *Administration,* XXIII, 2 (1975), 126-43.

Raven, John   "Some Results from Pilot Survey of Attitudes, Values' and Perceptions of Socio-Institutional Structures in Ireland". *Economic and Social Review,* IV, 4 (1973), 553-88.

Whelan, Noel   "Reform (or Change) in the Irish Public Service 1969-75". *Administration,* XXIII, 2 (1975), 113-25.

Index